THE SPIRIT OF
THE SPANISH MYSTICS

THE SPIRIT OF THE SPANISH MYSTICS

An anthology of Spanish Religious Prose from the Fifteenth to the Seventeenth Century

chosen, translated and introduced by
KATHLEEN POND

LONDON
BURNS & OATES

NIHIL OBSTAT: HVBERTVS RICHARDS, S.T.L., L.S.S.
CENSOR DEPVTATVS
IMPRIMATVR: E. MORROGH BERNARD
VICARIVS GENERALIS
WESTMONASTERII: DIE VIII NOVEMBRIS MCMLVII

MADE AND PRINTED IN GREAT BRITAIN BY
WILLIAM CLOWES AND SONS, LIMITED, LONDON AND BECCLES
FOR BURNS OATES AND WASHBOURNE, LTD
28 ASHLEY PLACE, LONDON, S.W.1

INTRODUCTION

WITH certain well-known exceptions, such as the writings of St. Teresa and St. John of the Cross, the 'Spiritual Exercises' of St. Ignatius and Rodriguez' 'On Christian Perfection', Spanish religious classics of the Golden Age and earlier are little read in this country, chiefly, perhaps, because in most cases they are not available in translation.

Spain is a country of realism, of intensity; and also a country of contrasts. It is outstanding among those European countries in which the roots of Catholicism have penetrated most deeply. It is true that revolutions and civil wars there have sometimes attacked the Church, but such attacks were not because men did not believe in Catholicism, but because they did—and for the moment were not prepared to surrender to it. The Spanish outlook on life is essentially that of the Faith, a preoccupation with the spiritual to the neglect, sometimes, of the material, a refusal to shrink from the stark reality of death, as, for instance, in the dying Cervantes' farewell to his friends: 'Farewell, graces, farewell, jests, farewell, my merry friends; I go on my way a-dying and soon I hope to see you all happy in the life to come'—the concern with honour, whatever sacrifice it may involve, the placing of truthfulness and honesty above self-interest and, perhaps least common of all in these days, respect for the human person as made in the image of Christ. The Spanish beggar, knowing that you believe he is made in God's image, sincerely believes he is conferring a favour upon you in asking you for alms, since he is offering you an opportunity of performing a work of charity, and so of coming closer to God. It is not, then, surprising, or should not be, that in Spain there should be a flowering of mysticism which seems to be unparalleled elsewhere,[1] for it is a country where people do not shrink from paying the price for spiritual experience.[2]

Spain, as has been said, is a land of contrasts. Just as it does not

[1] I have not forgotten England and the Low Countries, but, though considerable, the movement would seem to have been less widespread than in Spain.

[2] Some authorities estimate the number of writers on mysticism at more than 3,000.

consist exclusively of arid, treeless plains and wind-swept sierras—where the wind is so keen that it will kill a man though so thin that it may fail to put a candle out—so its religious literature is not wholly mystical. Much of it, parts of St. Teresa's writings, for instance, and Fray Luis de León's 'Perfect Wife', is concerned with the homely virtues. Much of it, again, is not directly concerned with man, but with God, so that it may be said to be mystical in the wide sense. Com-passion over the sufferings of Christ in his Passion—love of his Mother, love of the Sacrament of the Eucharist in which he both offers himself in sacrifice for us and gives himself to us, are themes which we find in the *Abecedario* of Francisco de Osuna.

In an anthology such as this, the choice of extracts cannot but be to some extent arbitrary. All that is claimed is that each passage is Spanish religious prose. The book has been arranged chronologically and each extract is prefaced by a short biographical notice of the author. It might have been compiled by grouping the subjects together, or again, by grouping the passages under the different religious Orders (though not all the writers quoted are members of such Orders). There is, perhaps, a good deal to be said for all three arrangements, and not more for one than for another. Of set purpose very little has been selected from writers already well known in this country, so that at first sight the few pages given to St. Teresa or St. John of the Cross, whose works are available in English in the late Professor Allison Peers' definitive translation,[1] may appear inadequate. Similarly, only a very brief extract has been given from the 'Exercises' of St. Ignatius. The 'Third Spiritual Alphabet' of Osuna was translated into English by a Benedictine of Stanbrook in 1931, but is now out of print. A translation of the third book of Laredo's 'Ascent of Mount Sion' was made by Professor Allison Peers shortly before his death. Rodriguez' 'Christian Perfection' is well known in religious houses in this country. Some few of the extracts here given are only available in Spanish in early printed editions. In the choice of passages, as many phases of spirituality as possible have been covered.

In the many quotations from Scripture which occur in the book, such borrowings as are indirect have been rendered directly from the Spanish, the homely style sometimes striking one as more

[1] St. Teresa, 'Complete Works', translated by E. Allison Peers, Sheed & Ward, London, 1946. St. John of the Cross, 'Complete Works', translated by E. Allison Peers, Burns Oates, London, 1950 (revised edition).

forceful just because it is new. Where possible, direct quotations have been given from the Knox version, but in cases where this has differed widely from the Spanish text, quotation has been made from the Douai (in this case D follows the reference). Phrases in square brackets have been added by the compiler in the hope of elucidating the Spanish text. Some of the better-known writers' names appear in English dress; the majority are given in their Spanish form.

It only remains for me to thank, as I do most sincerely, the friends who have been so kind as to help me with this book— Father Conrad Pepler, O.P., and Father J. D. Crichton for encouragement when the work was first planned and the latter for having read through and revised a portion of the manuscript; Father Walter Gumbley, O.P., F.R.H.S., for verifying an historical point; Father Guillermo Tejón, O.P., for help with one or two difficult pieces of translation, and Mr. Justin Gosling, B.A., B.Phil., for his kindness in reading the manuscript and for many helpful suggestions.

KATHLEEN POND

Oxford,
St. Gregory's Day, 1957

CONTENTS

GARCÍA DE CISNEROS
(1455-1510)

García de Cisneros, O.S.B., Abbot of Montserrat, was born at Cisneros in the diocese of León. He was a cousin of the famous Cardinal de Cisneros, compiler of the Polyglot Bible. García was probably a student at the university of Salamanca, but, surprisingly perhaps, since he was of noble family, nothing is known of his childhood or his studies. In 1470 (1475 according to one authority), he entered the Benedictine priory at Valladolid, outstanding at that time for the austerity of its observance. An eager student, Cisneros made a deep study of the psalms, of the sermons of St. Bernard, of certain writings of St. Bonaventure, and of Thomas à Kempis, Gerson, Gerard of Zutphen and others. In 1493 the priory at Valladolid was absorbed in the abbey of Montserrat and in 1496 García de Cisneros became prior and in 1499, abbot. He played an important part in the reform of the Spanish Benedictines. In 1496, before he had become abbot, he was sent by the Catholic Sovereigns to negotiate the peace with the King of France. He never enjoyed good health and, worn out with his labours and mortifications, died at the end of November 1510. He was immediately given the title of Venerable.

The *Ejercitatorio de la Vida Espiritual*, from which the present extracts are taken, was first published at Montserrat in 1500, the Spanish version of the Latin original being made by the monks of the abbey. The work shows the influence of the *Devotio Moderna* of the Brethren of Common Life, and is a symposium of extracts from Flemish writers (such as those mentioned above) on the life of prayer, edited and rearranged by Cisneros.

OF TWO MANNERS OF SILENCE AND SOLITUDE
Ch. 39 of *Ejercitatorio de la Vida Espiritual*
('An Exercise of the Spiritual Life')

Although men live in very different circumstances and conditions, it is possible for everyone to choose for himself some place apart to which he may withdraw to enjoy peace and silence. It is true, however, that dwelling apart and in silence must take place chiefly within the soul rather than externally. This means that the soul must cast out from herself and her dwelling-place every human and worldly care, every vain and harmful thought, and all other things likely to prevent her from reaching the goal she desires. It can

1

happen that a person may sometimes be physically alone and set apart from men, yet for all that is none the less subject to fancies, wandering thoughts and melancholy, and his own company is then most burdensome and troublous to him. Such fancies breed delirium in him and much useless working of the imagination, which represents to him first one thing and then another. It takes him at one moment into the kitchen, at another to the market, and brings before him unclean and carnal delights, showing him at one time dances and physical beauty, then songs and vanities of that sort, and draws him to sin and evil. St. Jerome humbly confesses this of himself, for although in the desert he had no company but that of wild beasts and scorpions, yet he sometimes found his imagination wandering back to the dances and the company of the ladies of Rome. In the same way fancies such as these cause the soul who is alone to vent her fury on someone who is absent and to contrive a quarrel with him and abuse him as if he were present. At other times such a person will count his money or, in imagination, carry on some business transaction, making a large profit. On other occasions his longings take him across the sea or on travels through different lands. At other times he sees himself raised to great dignities—and thus, in short, he is often full of similar fancies and innumerable absurdities.

The soul who is in this condition is dwelling neither apart nor in solitude, although she may be alone outwardly; but the devout soul who is active in contemplation is certainly not solitary, for she is never less alone than when so engaged. But the absence connected with the one state of solitude is quite different from that of the other. The devout, contemplative soul is not lonely, because through her holy desires and devout and holy thoughts, she has good, profitable and delightful company, namely, that of God and his saints. The other person, that is, the soul that is an aimless gadabout, frequents company that is harmful and makes use of nothing that is to her profit.

THAT IT IS NOT PRIDE TO ENGAGE IN THE SPIRITUAL LIFE, AS SOME THINK. (*Ejercitatorio*, ch. 42)

According to Gerson, it should not be said that he who takes the end of contemplation to be the loving of God deeply with one's whole heart is aiming too high or acting presumptuously in the matter. On the contrary, if anyone has the gift for so doing and has obtained this grace from God, he would be to blame and would act less perfectly, as we can see, if he did not use this gift of God, more especially if he were an ecclesiastic or a religious, for the life of such men is ordained to this end and in every way they have to give more to the contemplative than to the active life—otherwise their learning would not help them as clerics, especially if they were theologians, but would make them conceited and they would become vain, empty and proud. The same thing may be seen by a different example. Supposing there is at the royal court a kitchen servant whom the king wants to honour in a particular way. Let us suppose he wants to make him his steward, because he considers him fitted for the office and because it pleases the king to do so—it is beyond question that if this servant were to refuse the office on account of his laziness or faintheartedness, or through greed and gluttony, saying that it pleased him better to be in the kitchen, he would be very blameworthy. Similarly, he who can serve God in a life which is excellent would be not a little to blame if he were always to want to busy himself with lower things, and he would not be excusable on the grounds of humility—his action would rather be imputed to insincerity or want of real fervour. In the same way I say that those who in their contemplation seek to satisfy curiosity are at fault and err. What such people greatly need is humility, which guards charity itself, setting it ablaze anew.

HOW DEVOUT CONTEMPLATIVES NEED FIRM PERSEVERANCE TO REACH THE HEIGHT OF CONTEMPLATION. (*Ejercitatorio*, ch. 61)

He who thinks he can reach the height of contemplation or have the perfect warmth of divine love without firm perseverance is like a man who climbs a high mountain and, before he has reached the top, turns round to come down again on account of some difficulty or obstacle he meets with.

Such a man, moreover, may be compared to one who kindles a fire in green or rotting wood and, because it does not catch straight away, or because he sees nothing but smoke or some slight flame which can easily be extinguished, gets angry and puts it out, scattering the wood in all directions.

Or, he is like a man who cannot wait calmly for the wheat he has sown to ripen, or for the tree which he planted to strike its roots into the earth—and this because of the delay, danger or difficulty which he sees.

Or again he is like the monkey who longs to taste the green nut and, finding the shell bitter, gives up eating it and flings it away and so never gets to the sweetness of the kernel.

Finally, he may be compared to the slothful knight who, before the besieged city is completely taken, loses courage on account of the vexations and hardships, and goes away.

Do you see, then, brother, how a man acting in this manner fails to reach the heights of contemplation? Using these illustrations, he will be incapable of having the fire, or the wheat, or the tree, or the good flavour of the kernel, neither will he be able to reach the city. So, similarly, no one can come to the perfection of contemplation without firm perseverance.

DIONISIO VÁZQUEZ
(1479-1539)

Dionisio Vázquez, an Augustinian friar, was born in Toledo. He studied first in Spain, perhaps at Salamanca, and afterwards in Rome. He preached not only in his native country but in Italy, where his sermons were admired by Pope Leo X. He was the best preacher of the day and the one whom the Emperor Charles V most loved to hear. On one occasion Charles, worn out with fatigue, went on foot to hear Fray Dionisio and stood through the sermon lest he should fall asleep.

When Fray Vázquez was fifty-two, a Chair of Sacred Scripture was created for him at the university of Alcalá de Henares, so great was the esteem in which he was held by scholars. Crowds flocked to his lectures. Several times he was offered a bishopric, but each time refused. In the last years of his life, Fray Dionisio was afflicted with paralysis of the tongue. He accordingly resigned his Chair and retired to his monastery at Toledo. There is a great similarity between his sermons and those of Blessed John of Ávila. Among his other writings, Vázquez translated the *Martyrologium Romanum* into Spanish. He produced several Latin works, including a commentary on St. John's Gospel and a life of Christ.

NOTES FOR A SERMON ON THE ASSUMPTION

The Virgin was always holy, but she was also wearied with her sufferings in this life. If you consider her feasts you will see in them her sanctity and you will also see sufferings which will call forth your compassion. Her conception was holy, but to come into this world and enter the narrow confines of the womb is a matter for compassion. Her birth was holy, but she was born weeping like other children. In all her feasts you will always find something to excite your compassion for her. This feast, however, is of a new and different kind—because as in her lifetime her holiness was always accompanied by trials—since she was the holiest of all mankind she had most to suffer—so today, she who is holy, as she always was, is utterly free from suffering.

'She hath chosen the best part.'[1] It may seem strange that, since the Blessed Virgin is so great as to be worthy of whatever praise we can give her, she is today praised by the lips of our Lord

[1] From the Gospel of the former Mass for the Assumption.

5

'because she hath chosen the best part'.[1] It would seem that that is such an obvious course that no one would do otherwise. He who can attain to wealth does not choose poverty, he who can obtain health . . . and so on. What Christ meant when he praised his Mother as having the great wisdom and virtue to choose the best part must be something other than worldly perfection. That which is termed the best must be something different, for not without purpose did the Lord utter those words which are the condemnation of the errors of the world—that what is highly esteemed before men is an abomination before God. These are the words of God and therefore true.

But I fear greatly that there are many people who do not believe this with sufficient firmness. Wretched and incredulous worldlings! Not only should we believe the words of God but his works, especially those which caused him so much suffering and travail. He did not utter the teaching which cost him so much in jest—he wants it to be believed and put into practice.

Tell us, Lord—when you came from heaven to earth to teach us, did you, by chance, choose the best part, fine apparel, honours and repose and all other things that the world calls best? Truly, brethren, if what the world calls best and what it chooses *is* the best, Jesus Christ was deceived and chose the worst, whereas it is certain that *he* cannot be deceived. Let the world look at what he does and how he judges things and understand that God cannot be mistaken. Since he chose poverty and suffering, that *is* the best, and the contrary, however much the world chooses and esteems it, is the worst. As the Holy Virgin was taught by the Spirit of her Son even before he became incarnate, she did not fall into error, but chose the truth of God in preference to the falsehood of the world. You know quite well that whereas she could have been rich, she became poor, and having the right never to undergo suffering, for she was sinless, she was more exercised in it than any creature, however sinful. If you were to ask how she had the heart to choose poverty and sacrifice for God in preference to the pleasures that the world considers fit for the gods, I would say that her knowledge and love of God were so great, so great the esteem in which she held him, that to attain him, and that in the greatest possible degree, not only did she not desire earthly things, but she would not even take them if they were given to her, holding it for certain that the more she left for God, the more she would receive from him. For this reason, much more than St. Paul, she esteemed all things as dung, because God was precious in her eyes. No one should mind that the things of this world are called dung, for the world was not created for man but as a dwelling for beasts; such a place is called a stable and what there is in it is dung. Soulless people, shrivelled in heart, and clinging to what is low! Why do you go about restless, harassed and, as it were, dead, striving to swell your coffers and your bosoms with the vilest dung, whereas you could give your love to eternal goods which surpass anything that your desire can realize? O Virgin, blessed for ever, there was no room in you for smallness of heart, for even the very aspiration to be a virgin is largeness of heart since it means spurning and trampling underfoot our flesh, that mighty enemy, by which many, both small and great, are miserably overcome. A great enterprise was this and the first woman to undertake it was the Mother of God, and therefore she is called Virgin of virgins. As she undertook it with greatness of heart, so she persevered in it and came out victorious.

But her large-heartedness did not stop at this. She did not only show it in despising the flesh and all the world (and if I were to say all heaven, too, I should not lie), but set herself, as the Gospel says, to choose the best part of all, namely God, who is far above the sum total of all other good, for he is goodness integral and complete, so much so that in comparison the holiness of the saints is not holiness, light is darkness, and all goods joined together are nothing. It is here, men, that you should set your eyes, that they may become enamoured of that beauty; set your heart here. Learn from this holy woman who was so taught that she chose the best part of all and displayed such skill in seeking it that she obtained it and possesses it for ever and it will not be taken away from her. All this David saw in spirit in praise of this our Lady. 'What have I in heaven besides thee . . .' O faithful love! O loving fidelity, devoted to that which, since it is the supreme good, is worthy that love should leave all other objects and fix itself on him. 'What have I to desire in heaven?' says the Virgin. For although there are there things of such great excellence that beyond compare they surpass those of earth, so great is the measure by which God surpasses them that, for anyone who understands this as the Blessed Virgin understood it, they are as nothing, unworthy, hindering the love which should flow towards God. If the Holy Virgin does not turn her head at the things there are in heaven, nor even look at them lest she should cloud the vision with which

she contemplates God, and lest she should hold back even a tiny
part of her heart's love (for she holds it a great evil not to give to
God her heart whole and entire), how much less account will she
make of the things of earth, since they are of so little value? The
heart of the Virgin was truly poor in respect of them all. She read
and put into practice what the Lord most high said: 'Thou hast
wounded my heart, my sister.' So great was her thirst for God,
not only in her soul but even bodily, as David says, that her flesh
and her heart failed her, and thus she fulfilled more completely than
any creature what is said in Scripture: 'Daughters of Jerusalem I
adjure you, because I languish with love.'[1] But this malady is
health and he who does not suffer from this sickness is ill indeed.

If his father's honour suffers it is shameful, one of the most
blameworthy attitudes there can well be in a son, to esteem that
honour as of little worth; if the son is rich and allows his father to
suffer poverty; if, possessing abundance, he allows him to die of
hunger; if he is prosperous and allows him to go badly dressed—
this is a great failure of sonship. Christ our Redeemer did not fall
into this fault with his most holy Mother, nor permit that in her
there should be any lack or anything at all by which she might be
put to shame; rather he honoured her with such great favours that
all in earth and heaven confess and hold her as queen and lady. If
some day the Son is to show us mercy, it will be in her . . . .

One of the greatest martyrdoms the Blessed Virgin suffered was
loneliness, for she was seeking Christ in the whole course of her
life and especially so from the Resurrection until her assumption.
Mothers experience something of this when their sons are absent
for a long time. Consider, then, what such a Mother would feel,
absent from such a Son. It cannot be expressed, nor felt, nor
written; nor even do I think that you will believe this when I try
to tell you, for we have not given much time to speaking of this.
You should know, then, that God gives divine love to whom he
wills and when he wills, and in the measure he wills, such that, for
the time it lasts, there is no greater torment than to find oneself
upon earth. Neither do such people take comfort in gardens, nor
in houses, nor in all the rest that gives delight, rather all this they
consider a reproach and it displeases them; and if great difficulties
and perils through which they must go to God were placed in their
way, they would go to meet them with as much determination and
courage as others would to things of great honour. David under-

1 For this and the preceding quotation, cf. Canticle of Canticles 2:5, 7 and
4:9 [D].

stood this very well. 'My soul hath thirsted for thee.'[1] David was a king and was occupied in much business; he ruled the kingdom carefully and provided what was necessary. With all this he said that his soul was so much on fire and wounded with the love of God that nothing could give him coolness and refreshment until he found himself wholly submerged in the waters of grace. We, with the name and function and obligation of being recollected and spiritual persons, are upon earth, and yet have not the slightest sorrow at finding ourselves without God, a clear sign that we have very little love for him. If David said that, you should lift up your thoughts when you can, trying to realize what she who was God's Mother, and who loved God incomparably more than David did, would feel and say. What would her heart not suffer when, as she prayed the *Pater noster*, she said 'Thy kingdom come', and felt in herself such exceeding eagerness and desire for the accomplishment of the kingdom of God. In this desire the following petition 'Thy will be done' would come before her. For you it is a small thing to say this, for you have little or perhaps no desire to see the kingdom of God. But the Blessed Virgin, who desired it so much, suffered great martyrdom in pronouncing this petition because when an angel showed her his kingdom life was torture to her, and her desire was to see herself loosed from the bonds of the flesh, yet despite all this her prayer to God was: 'Since it serves your purpose that things be thus, *fiat voluntas tua*.'

[1] Cf. Psalm 62:2.

ANTONIO DE GUEVARA, BISHOP
OF MONDOÑEDO
(c. 1480–1545)

Antonio de Guevara came of a noble family from the Asturias. At the early age of twelve, we hear of him at court where he was possibly a page in the service of Prince John, only son of Isabel the Catholic. On the queen's death (1504), he became a Franciscan friar. He held important positions in his Order, being Guardian in turn at the houses of Ávila, Arévalo and Soria, and, later, Inquisitor at Toledo and Valencia. We read of his accompanying Charles V on his Italian journeys and he was preacher, counsellor and chronicler to the emperor. He travelled much and far afield on imperial business, visiting Germany, Rome, Genoa, Florence and Venice, and England. In both Rome and Naples he took part in public controversy with the Jews. As bishop, first of Guadix, near Granada, and later of Mondoñedo, Guevara endowed many hospitals and schools and founded a printing press. He died at Valladolid in 1545.

Among Guevara's writings may be mentioned a book on the duties of princes (*Reloj de Príncipes*), widely read, the *Menosprecio de corte y alabanza de aldea*[1] and a number of minor works. He is perhaps best known for his *Epístolas familiares* from which the present extracts are taken.

'MY YOKE IS SWEET'[2]
(from *Epístolas familiares*)

[Letter IV to the Count of Miranda, in which the saying of Christ, 'My yoke is sweet', is explained. It is one of the most important letters that Guevara wrote.]

Illustrious Lord and royal steward: In your letter you tell me to send you in the Spanish tongue the explanation of that saying of Christ: 'My yoke is sweet and my burden light' which you heard me preaching to His Majesty the other day in the sermon for All Saints. You say you were enraptured at hearing it and would like very much to have it. You also write me that it will not be much for me to take the trouble to send you the explanation of that saying, for you came to see me when I was guardian at Soria—so that if I did not want to do it out of goodwill, you would ask me for it as a matter of justice. I do not want to deny that that visit

---

1 'Contempt of Court and praise of rustic Life'.   2 Matthew 11:30.

was a very great favour and consolation to me, for the monastery is damp and the place cold, the air keen, the bread scarce, the wine bad, the water hard and the people by no means slow-witted; for in truth if elsewhere they judge according to what they see, there they say what they think. What I felt most there was not the lack of provisions but the absence of friends, without whom there is no place on earth which pleases, nor conversation which satisfies. You are quite right, my Lord, to plead the visit you made and the consolation you gave me; for the good friend can do no greater thing for his friend than to remedy his necessities and console him in tribulation. If I want to show you kindness in return for such a great favour, I am not a lord; if I want to serve you, I have not the wherewithal; if I want to visit you, I have no liberty; if I want to pay you, I am poor; and if I want to give you something, you do not need it. What I can do is to acknowledge the favour you did me then and to comply with what you order me to do now. Although this may seem little, you should not regard it as little that I look upon you as my Lord and call you my friend, for to thank you for the kindly benefit received is really much more than to pay it back to you. Vice for vice, malice for malice, and evil for evil, there is not a man in this world so evil as the ungrateful man—hence it is that the heart which is tender and human forgives all injuries except ingratitude, which it never forgets. From Alexander the Great in conferring favours and Julius Caesar in forgiving injuries—down to the present day, two princes who surpassed or even equalled them have yet to be born—yet we read of them that if they knew that a man was ungrateful, Alexander gave him nothing nor did Caesar pardon him.

Explanation of ' My yoke is sweet'.

As to what you say, my Lord, that I should send you what I preached to His Majesty just as I preached it, that is a thing I am never accustomed to do, nor even ought to do; for if it is in our power to send you what we say, we cannot send you the grace with which we preach it; because the blessing which God gives to the tongue at that particular hour, he seldom gives afterwards power to the pen. Aesculapius among the Argives, Demosthenes among the Athenians, Aeschines among the inhabitants of Rhodes, and Cicero among the Romans, not only knew how to declaim but were even princes among orators. Despite this, no speech which they declaimed to the public were they afterwards willing

to give in writing, for they said that they did not want to entrust
to the pen the glory which their tongue had created. To go from
the plan to the house, from the model to the building, from the
figure to what is figured and from the natural to what is represented,
is the same as going from hearing a sermon in the pulpit to reading
it afterwards in writing; for on what is written only the eyes are
fixed, but with the spoken word the heart is lifted up. It is a quality
of divine letters that when read they lend themselves to understanding and when heard to appreciation with relish; whence it is
that many more persons are turned to God by the sermons that
they hear than by the books they read. I, my Lord, want to do what
you order me and send you what you ask me for, but I ask for a
promise and make a protestation that, if it does not seem as good
to you when you read it as it did when you heard it, you do not
blame my charity, but your importunity.

Coming, then, to the point—Christ says: 'Come to me all you
who are burdened and heavy-laden, and I will relieve and refresh
you'. Isaias says in his visions: '*Onus Babilonis, onus Moab, onus
in Arabia, onus Aegipti, onus Damasci, onus deserti maris, onus Tiri*';
which means: 'I saw Babylon burdened, Moab burdened, Arabia
burdened, Egypt burdened, Damascus burdened, Tyre burdened'.
The prophet David says: '*Sicut onus grave gravatum est super me*';[1]
as if he were to say—'they threw a very heavy burden upon me.'
It may be gathered from what we have said that before Christ, all
the old law was heavy, painful, leaving us burdened and even
suffering, for it was severe with those who transgressed. As reward
for the moral precepts they observed, the legal obligations they
carried out, the ceremonial rites they performed and the sacrifices
they offered, God gave victory over their enemies, peace to the
state, health to individuals, and wealth with which they could keep
up their houses but no more. What greater burden could there be
in the world than that he who broke the law should go straight to
hell and that he who kept it should not be given paradise immediately? From the time the old law began until it came to a
close, men continually heaped precept upon precept, ceremony
upon ceremony, law upon law, burden upon burden, and even
suffering upon suffering: so that all sought to impose burdens and
none to alleviate them. The first in the world to proclaim that all
those burdened should come to him and he would relieve them,
all those heavily laden that he might take away their load, was

[1] Psalm 37:5.

Christ our God, and this was when that law of fear dissolved in the crucible of love.

It should be noted here that any yoke is of its nature heavy, harsh, hard and painful and the animal who carries it goes along bound and burdened. Christ says on the other hand, that his yoke is sweet to bear and his burden light to carry, a thing that is certainly worth understanding and a thought which lifts us up to God. Christ did not simply say that any yoke is sweet; for otherwise we should not know of what yoke he was speaking, nor even what law he approved. In saying that his yoke is sweet, Christ gives us to understand that the other yokes are bitter: in saying that his burden was light, he let it be understood that the others were heavy: so that he relieves us when he burdens us and frees us when he places a yoke upon us. Neither did Christ say: 'My yokes are sweet and my burdens are light'—for God neither commands us to plough with many yokes, nor to burden ourselves with many burdens. It is the devil who persuades us to fall into many vices, the world which submerges us in much business, the flesh which demands from us much indulgence; for the good Christ our God does not ask of us more than to love him and not hate our brothers. The law of the Hebrews was a law of fear, but the law of Christians is a law of love, and as the former served God by force and we do so willingly, that law is called hard and the law of Christ sweet. The property of love is that the rough becomes smooth, the cruel gentle, the bitter sweet, the insipid savoury, the irritating soothing, the malicious simple, the dull alert, and even the heavy light. He who loves is incapable of murmuring against those persons who annoy him, nor does he refuse what is asked of him, nor resist their taking it, nor answer when they would quarrel with him, nor take revenge when they affront him, nor even go away if they dismiss him. What does he forget who loves with all his heart? What does he who is wholly taken up by love leave undone? Of what does he who never ceases to love complain? If he who loves has some complaint, it is not of that which he loves, but of himself that he has fallen somewhat short of the love with which he was striving to serve. Oh what a great thing it would be if, since we are Christians, we were in love with the law of Christ, for truly in that case we should neither go about wistful, nor live sorrowful! For the heart that is taken up with love neither flees from dangers, nor faints in its labours.

The yoke that the animals bear, when it is new is in itself very heavy, but when it has become dry and has been borne for a time, it is softer to bear and lighter to carry! O good Jesus! O God, what high mystery! You did not will to burden us with the yoke of your law immediately, but upon becoming man took it upon yourself and first, for thirty years, bore it yourself, in order that it might be drained [of its bitterness], and become light and smooth. What did Christ order us to do that he did not first do himself? What yoke did he put upon us without first carrying it upon his shoulders? If he commands us to fast, he fasted; if he commands us to pray, he prayed; if he orders us to forgive, he forgave; if he bids us die, he died; and if he bids us love, he loved; so that if he commands us to take medicine, he first underwent the experience himself. Christ does not compare his blessed law to wood, nor to stone, nor to the plants, nor to iron, but only to the yoke; for all these things only one can bear, but the yoke has to be pulled by the force of two. This is a very deep and profound mystery, through which it is given us to understand that in the hour when the good Christian lowers his neck beneath the yoke to carry it, immediately Christ puts himself on the other side of him to help him. No one calls on Christ without his answering; no one recommends himself to him, whom he does not succour; no one asks of him, to whom he does not give something; no one serves him without his rewarding them; and no one labours whom he does not help. The yoke of the law of Christ rather feigns to wound than wounds, pardons rather than chastises, excuses rather than accuses, frightens perhaps but does not weary, and even rather relieves than burdens; for the very Christ who bids us bear it, himself and no other, helps us to carry it.

Good Jesus! Love of my soul! With a leader like you, who will lose the way? With a patron like you, who fears to be overwhelmed? With a captain like you, who will despair of victory? With a companion like you, what yoke is there that is burdensome? Gentle law! Happy yoke! The labour we undergo for you, O Christ, is well employed! For not only do you glory in being present in the midst of our labours, but you promise not to leave us alone. He who in the garden of Gethsemane went out to receive those who were going to arrest him—we can well believe will go out to embrace those who come to serve him. If a rich worldling wants to take up arms against a poor Christian, we shall find in truth that the precious aid that Christ gives to those who serve him is greater far than the protection the world gives to those who follow it. To those whom the world drags beneath its yoke, all things are given calculated, measured and weighed; but in the house of God all is given whole, entire, without demanding its

price, and in measure full to overflowing. With good reason can
we say that the yoke of Christ is sweet and his burden very light,
for the world does not even pay us for the services we do it and
Christ pays us even for the good thoughts we have of him. Christ
knows well that of our nature we are weak, wretched, dull and
indolent, for which reason he does not consider us as we are, but
as we would be. Moses gave a law to the Hebrews, Solon to the
Greeks, Foroneus to the Egyptians and Numa Pompilius to the
Romans. As men made these laws, they came to an end as men come
to an end, but the yoke of the law of God will last as long as God
lasts. What can the law of Moses, in which divorce and usury were
permitted, be worth? What could the law of Foroneus, in which
the Egyptians were permitted to become robbers, be worth? The
law of Lycurgus, in which homicide was not punished? The law
of Solon, by which adultery was practised? The law of Numa
Pompilius, in which men were allowed to seize as much as they
could take? What was the law of the Lydians worth in which
maidens had no other marriage than that they won by adultery?
What could be the value of the Balearic law, in which it was
commanded that they should not hand over the bride to the
bridegroom until the nearest relative knew her carnally? We cannot
but say that these and other similar laws were bestial, brutal and
unchaste, for in them were contained vices which men were
permitted to practise. He who enters the religion of Christ to be a
Christian is not permitted to be proud, a thief, a homicide, an
adulterer, gluttonous, malicious or blasphemous, and if it should
happen that we should see someone who behaves as such, he
merely tarnishes the name of Christian for in all things else he will
be a citizen of hell. The sacred law of Christ is so upright in what
it admits and so pure in what it permits that it neither suffers vice,
nor makes compromise with the vicious man; 'For the law of the
Lord is pure'.[1] The Jews and the Arabs, the pagans and gentiles,
who defame our law and complain of its harshness, are certainly
wrong, nor even have they excuse for speaking as they do, for the
defect is not that it is bad, but that it is badly kept by us. Those
who want to be virtuous will never find Christ's precepts harsh;
for the yoke of God is not for those who follow their own opinion
but for those who live in conformity with reason. Finally I say that
all we do as Christians, we were obliged to do if we would regard
ourselves as men, and therefore Christ says that his yoke is sweet

[1] Psalm 18:1 [D].

and his burden light; for he is so good and so generous that he rewards us for what we do for him as if we were not obliged to do it.

This then is what I think about this saying and this is what I said to His Majesty when I preached before him. No more, except may our Lord keep you, and give me his grace that I may serve him.

Madrid, 1st June, 1526.

THAT MONASTIC LIFE IS TO BE PREFERRED TO THE COURT
(from *Epístolas familiares*, Letter XXVIII)

To the Abbot of Montserrat

Very Reverend and dear Abbot:

[The letter begins with acknowledgments of previous correspondence and then gives a reply to a question the Abbot had evidently put, on the subject of pagan oratories.]

I remember having been to the shrine of Our Lady of Loreto, of Our Lady of Guadalupe, of the Rock of France [Rocamadour], of the grotto at Segovia and at Balvaneya, which are all shrines and sanctuaries of much prayer and greatly venerated; but for my pleasure, and for my own taste, I find Our Lady of Montserrat to be a building worthy of admiration, a temple of prayer and a shrine of devotion. I tell you in very truth, father Abbot, that never did I find myself among those rugged peaks, those high mountains, those magnificent hills and those thick woods, without resolving to change my life, without grieving for my past, and without rejecting liberty and finding a love for solitude. Never do I visit Montserrat without immediately experiencing sorrow for sin, without making my confession, over which I take full time, without celebrating Mass with tears, without keeping vigil there one night, without giving something to the poor, without lighting blessed candles and, above all, without taking my fill of sighs and purposing to amend my life. Would that it should please the God of heaven and Our Lady of Montserrat that on this earth I might be such as I resolve to be when in that holy house! Alas, alas, father Abbot, the more days I live the weaker I feel myself in virtue, and what is worst of all is, that in good desires I am very holy, and in doing good works I am very remiss. Preaching as I do that heaven is full of good works and hell of good desires, I don't know if it is friends who advise me, relatives who importune me, enemies who turn me aside from the true path, business which comes my way, the emperor[1] who always keeps me occupied, or the devil who is always tempting me; for the more I resolve to separate myself from the world, the more—increasingly so each day—I sink down to the depths.

Can it be true, then, to say that the life of the Court is so peaceful, that one should desire it? On the contrary, there we suffer hunger, cold, thirst, weariness, poverty, sadness, annoyances, loss of favour and persecution; and all this we undergo because there is no one to take liberty away from us or to ask us for an account of our idleness. Believe me, father Abbot, do not doubt that for the soul and even for the body, the life you have there in Montserrat is much better than that we have here at Court. For as to the Court, it is much better to be an observer of what goes on in its precincts than an imitator. In the Court he who is worth little is forgotten, and he who is worth much is persecuted. At the Court the poor man has nothing to eat and the rich can make his importance felt. At the Court there are few who live content and many who find it wearisome. At the Court all strive after privilege, and in the end one man comes to command everything. At the Court no one wants to die and we see no one willing to leave it. At the Court many do what they want and few what they ought. At the Court, all the courtiers blaspheme and afterwards all others follow their example. Finally, I say and affirm what I have said and preached many times and that is, that the Court is only for favourites who enjoy it and for youths who do not realize what it is. If, with these conditions, father Abbot, you want to come to the Court, here and now I will exchange it for your Montserrat, and I even pledge you my faith as a Christian, that you will repent of having turned courtier more times than I of making myself a happy monk there. For the great love I bear you and for the devotion I have, be good enough to ask our Lord to take me away from this infamous life and to warm me with his grace, without which we cannot serve him or much less serve ourselves.

From the hand of Fr. Rodrigo I received the spoons which you sent me and to him I gave the book you asked me for; so that I have spoons to eat with and your paternity does not lack the Hours to pray. As to the rest that you write me about the monastery, you will pray God for me in your devotion, and vis-à-vis the emperor I will perform for you the office of a friend. No more, except may our Lord have you in his keeping.

At Valladolid, 7th January, 1535.

[1] i.e. Charles V.

BERNARDINO DE LAREDO
(1482–1540)

Bernardino of Laredo was born in 1482. It seems that when old enough he began his career as page to an exiled Portuguese nobleman, but soon abandoned the court and devoted himself to the study of medicine, beginning to practise as a physician in the year 1507. At the age of twenty-eight, however, Bernardino decided to enter the Franciscan Order as a lay-brother. He died in 1540 at a house of his Order at Villaverde, about twenty miles to the north-east of Seville.

Bernardino acted as apothecary in the religious houses to which he was assigned. On two occasions he is known to have attended royalty in his capacity as physician. He wrote two works on medicine, as well as the spiritual treatise for which he is so justly renowned, 'The Ascent of Mount Sion', originally published in 1535. Laredo afterwards revised this work, correcting its theology where necessary, for when he first wrote, his theological knowledge cannot have been more than superficial. A further edition was published in Valencia in 1590, long after Laredo had passed to his reward, emended by a Dominican, Fr. Jerome Acoceri, S.T.M. The text of this latter edition has been used for the present extracts.

The work is divided into three parts, the first treating of self-knowledge, the second of the following of Christ and the third of the worship of God in contemplation. The late Professor Allison Peers published a translation of and commentary on Part 3, shortly before his death.[1] If Laredo's style is sometimes difficult, the matter of 'The Ascent' is worthy to be compared with the mystical writings of Osuna and others, and all three parts of the book repay careful study.

THAT THE CROSS IS THE DOOR BY WHICH
WE ENTER INTO LOVE
(from 'The Ascent of Mount Sion', Part I)

For a man to make progress in the ways of prayer, there is no other method than to go to God with love, for there are more opportunities of loving him than ways of doing so, and more ways than there are lovers. To enter into this love, there is no entrance like that door which is the cross of Jesus Christ, our dearest Lord.

[1] Bernardino of Laredo: *The Ascent of Mount Sion*, London, 1952.

It is fitting that the cross should enter the soul and the body be placed upon it if its strength permits. The soul who desires to enter directly through this door has to try to be detached from the body as regards sensuality, for he who will lose his life here is to find it in life eternal. The first steps in life eternal are the entering in through this door—for if eternal life is Christ, he is the keeper of that door and stands before the entrance, holding the keys, which are of hard iron, in his hands. Since the cross is the door for entering into love and love is the keeper of the door, it is clear that this grace is close at hand; for the love of God is Christ, and from Christ is the love of God, and God's love and God are simply one all-pervading God, whom the contemplative seeks, entering into Christ's humanity, when he wants to find him, through the door of wood.

Here there remains something which I do not explain, for I cannot express it. But the cross is mighty in Christ crucified in whom is my remedy. I am in the presence of the God of immensity, who knows the thoughts which he puts into the heart of his fugitive slave, in the innermost places of his soul. It is certain that the soul which tries to enter into herself will find God in a secret enclosure and can there remain with him if she will. But to enjoy God she has to find the courage to learn to say that the temple should be destroyed and she will build it up again in three days. For the destruction six workmen are needed. They will dig until the foundation trenches are well deepened, and will then turn over and break up all loose earth in order that the foundations may not be made upon that, so that one may not labour uselessly since the form of the building is not yet perfected—just as we see that those waste their labour who want to erect walls without making a proper foundation. The more dangerous such walls are, the higher they presume to raise them. When the foundation trench is opened up, having due regard to the loose earth mentioned above, the building can then be finished in three days.

On the first day the foundation stone is firmly set, because the temple must be built upon firm stone. When the soul looks for the wounds in her wretched body, and realizes who she is and whence and which way she came, what she is carrying and where she is going, then, as is done by a skilful mason, with the labour of those six workmen a trench is opened in the building, the six workmen being six considerations. When a man has opened the trench of self-knowledge, he can now take the cross of our most sweet Christ and place it upon himself, and that is the foundation stone in this building of ours. When the cross of Christ goes into the soul, it is necessary that the body should try to mount the cross too. The cross enters into the soul by meditation and the body takes it upon itself by a strict and austere life. This will be the second day of the three mentioned by him who is making the foundations of this building of ours upon that firm rock.

Now the foundation has to be of limestone and sand, that is, a life that is strict and of continual austerity (except when, for my confusion, God allows my strength to fail); but also there must be mixed with it the bitter but reviving water of tears which comes from the trench of our knowledge if it is truly deep. Thus to the cutting and the foundation are assigned two days of the building, so that on the third day there may be well set as a keystone the stone which he, the builder, rejected without looking at it. This the soul does when she fixes her heart on the love of her God with full and determined intent (trusting in God's great goodness) to die a thousand times rather than separate herself from him, regretting the time spent without contemplating the perfection of this stone which perfects his temple so that she may thus rejoice in it in most sweet love.

Thus are the walls of Jerusalem built, when the Lord works his kindly will upon the soul which is Sion. It is a well-ordered temple and there the people of our mighty Lord come to take refuge, ease and shelter, in holy meditations, lively faith, hope and living charity and in unceasing desires. Thus is the people of the Lord.

In this temple God has placed his altar on which there are offered to him the calves of sighs and heartfelt groans. Here he accepts the sacrifices of penance, the oblations of examples communicated to others, and the holocaust of the loving soul's delicate offerings. Thus when the soul enters that building which her God has erected in her, and sees the harmony that the living God has set in her, she feels constrained to sing with ineffable joy, saying: 'Truly God is in this place and I was not aware of him'—being vexed with herself that she did not recognize her God, until he in his goodness ordered her to deepen the trench and made her foundation firm and perfected the work; here (always trusting in her God), she thinks she can live in the quietest repose, fearing her littleness and rejoicing with reverential fear, because she knows that this edifice is the tabernacle of the Lord of hosts, in the desire of whom, with much reason, the soul of the loving psalmist is said to faint. He truly served our most sweet Lord, as he invites others to serve him. May our most sweet Jesus Christ be our redeemer.

OF THE PRAYER, AGONY AND SWEAT OF CHRIST,
THE LAMB OF GOD
(from 'The Ascent of Mount Sion', Part II)

When Christ Jesus, who is our good, was praying in Gethsemane the day before his Passion, the dread instruments with which his boundless charity was to erect the building of our redemption at terrible cost were present to his humanity. In the provisions of his eternal wisdom, his most holy and suffering humanity recognized the rope that was to bind his delicate throat, the white garment with which they were to mock him, the scourges from which he was to receive five thousand four hundred and more stripes of immeasurable cruelty, the purple the instrument of his greatest reviling, the bandage which was to cover his eyes, the reed with which they were to mock him, the crown of thorns which was to pierce his most delicate head with cruel sharpness, all the jeers, the nails and the cross of immeasurable cruelty. Moreover, all the excruciating torments which he was to suffer severally and together were shown to him at once, and, in addition, he recognized the lance which, when he had expired, was to cleave in two within her crucified breast the warm, sensitive heart of his most sorrowful mother. He saw, together with this, the desertion of his dear company of well-beloved disciples. The torment of all this was so great, the pain so terrible and the suffering so piercing, that it absorbed Christ both body and soul into itself as it were. As the charity of that true man who was at the same time true God surpassed human understanding in the highest degree, the compassion his soul felt for his crucifiers who were not to be saved[1] was so great that the anguish of this compassion pierced his very heart to such an extent that it caused a sharp fire which was instantly keener in every part than the other pains which we have called sensitive.

The terrible intensity of this burning suffering was the chalice of bitterness which his humanity, aflame with immense charity in the divine love, asked the eternal Father that he might not have to taste. That is, he asked that since he was willing to suffer for us the torments he foresaw, they might not be unavailing for those whom he willed to be saved; but that those who were crucifying him were being lost was a chalice more bitter to him than the pain of his sufferings. Thus it was that he did not refuse to suffer the

---

[1] This seems an unwarranted assumption on Laredo's part.

Passion. And because his immeasurable love is equally as eternal as his infinite justice, he said: 'If it be possible'—as if he had said that the humanity which was being consumed in the fierce fire of his immense charity was ready to suffer, although the flesh, in so far as it is flesh, is weak, and the willing spirit desired that these his crucifiers might not perish, if that could be reconciled with eternal justice. Since in this last, anguished prayer there were present at one and the same time so many and such deep and extensive reasons of praying with intense fervour, it was necessary to prolong the interval of time, lengthening and drawing out the prayer.

And as the innocent victim of love prayed, he became more and more on fire with love, and so his entire being was aflame and his life-spirit stirred and drew to itself the natural heat of his sacred humanity, so that his pores opened and he was in agony and abundantly sweated the finest blood. It is to be noted that the Gospel says in this place, 'as it were drops of blood', and we refer this reading 'as it were' to the drops, so that we may understand it to mean 'as it were drops'. We can interpret it in this way, for it is still in conformity with the letter. But whether we say 'drops as it were, of blood' or 'drops of, as it were blood', even if it fits in better with compassionate love, as it does—we are not, because it says 'as it were', to fail to understand and truly believe that it was the finest blood. For blood in the usual meaning of the word, there is none outside the veins except in the heart; and the blood which is within the veins is not so cleansed, so pure nor so digested as that which issues by way of exudation through the pores, spreading through the limbs and every part of them, very close to all the pores and very ready to exude—so much so that medical doctors compare it to the dew there is on the leaves of the trees, very ready to issue forth at the faintest movement, however slight it may be. Because this blood is now outside the veins and is going to be converted into flesh, because it is finer, purified and more perfect, it is no longer known by the name of blood, as it was when in the veins, but immediately it has issued from them, spreading itself beneath the pores of this our human body, it should rather be called liquid[1] than blood. When it becomes thicker it is known as viscous liquid and when it is passing into the nature of flesh, we have the change of that liquid into flesh and all these three liquids, one less and another more, are very properly known as radical or fundamental moisture.

[1] i.e. 'humour' in the terminology of sixteenth-century science.

According to our way of thinking, the sweat of our most dear Jesus was not of blood from the veins, but from the very fine blood of the porous liquid, blood which is purer and more full of life, and which in man is spread over any and every one of the limbs beneath any of the pores, ready to issue forth when he wills that it shall be given place, or with the prick of a needle or of a very fine thorn, not sharp enough to break a vein, or through the opening of any pore. Since, then, in our most sweet Christ, his travail and anguish were so intense that they caused him to be in agony, which is to arrive at a point only a little removed from expiring—a little before he had said that his soul was sorrowful even to the point of death—and since this anguish was so all-pervading that it affected the whole of his most blessed soul most intensely and reached out to every part of his most suffering body, and throughout, the natural heat, stirred by the fire of the flame of divine charity, was active—all the pores over his whole body opened, and through each and every one of them he sweated very fine blood, purer than the blood from the blood-vessels.

This saying 'as it were blood' in this place denotes blood finer than the blood which flows in the veins. Wherefore it should be noted that for this reason there was no one who sweated blood before Christ or after him: because there has never been nor will be anyone who suffered such great anguish nor with so much love, for if that had been possible to such a man, the sweat of blood would also be possible and natural to him.

This we should note with all our compassion and it is even something that can be preached about. It may attract some preacher, for any good doctor will be able to confirm it quite easily. It is also clear that it is something of which many good and learned men do not think when they preach this mystery. If they are asked about the sweat of blood, although they give good reasons, they lack the proper knowledge of anatomy—which is not necessary for the reading of Sacred Scripture, but without it, the occasion of such a sweat cannot be grasped, nor of radical or fundamental moisture as being its known cause. And from the midst of his very heart, Jesus Christ our Lord, bids us ponder this well.

THE FASHIONING OF THE CITY OF GOD
(from 'The Ascent of Mount Sion', Part III)

Taking for granted, then, the foundation described in the two previous chapters, let us think of a field, smooth, even and pleasing to the eye, such that when the soul is set in the midst of it, all its parts are seen to be perfectly equal. Let us endeavour to surround it all with finest crystal, a fair and precious jewel. In each of the divisions or parts of that square, three towers wrought of precious stones are to be raised. So that this enclosure with its turrets will shut in the city, that it may be the holy city, the heavenly Jerusalem, whose walls, it is written, are of precious stones. If, then, there are four divisions and three towers to each, there will be twelve towers as will afterwards be seen. From the top of each of these towers are to be hung four shields of fine gold. The wall, then, is crystal, wonderfully clear, the towers of every kind of precious stone and the shields of fine gold. All this is now set in place.

In the midst of this field, now enclosed, which is an even-sided square, let us imagine that a rich paschal candle is lighted, whose wick is pure beyond all pureness, wrought in such perfection and made by such a skilled craftsman that when the candle is lighted, throughout space and time it is impossible for it to be consumed or diminished, or for its brightness to fail for any cause whatever. For the wax of this lighted candle is the most sacred body of Christ, the wick his most blessed soul, and in his light perfectly enkindled, we can all raise the mind to the most holy Trinity in its single and most pure substance. Thus in the essence of the light, the person of the Father is contemplated, through its radiance the soul is raised to the Son and through the light which is brightness itself, you can raise the mind to the Spirit, the Paraclete. It is no more than one substance, so single when it is all pure in that enkindled flame that it cannot be broken up, nor separated nor divided, because where the light is, there is its radiance, and where the radiance is, the light cannot be lacking; and from the radiance engendered from the light and the light which engendered, is now engendering and ever will engender the radiance of both with undivided equality, proceeds the brightness. It is not a single flame, but one which is threefold and without division.

Let the soul, then, return to the field, and let its imaginative faculty serve the understanding, and the understanding the will, so that the will may be quiet in God. Let us consider the lighted candle, the purity, perfection and majesty of which gives of itself such great light and such great brightness that it strives to pass through the wall and cast itself into the crystal and penetrate it through and through. As to the towers wrought of many and different very precious stones, it penetrates them all, making them living stones. The most intense brightness that there is now both within and without each of the stones, reverberates, passing into the crystal and reflecting back the clearness of the crystal in each one of the stones; the stones and the crystal in turn throw their reflection on to the shields. The shields reflect on to the crystal and the gems and thus each one of the precious stones participates in the brightness of the others and all of them in that of each singly, both of the crystal and the gold. The gold receives effulgent splendour from the precious stones and crystal and not even for an instant do they cease to flash back their own splendour, that is to reflect into one another and then reflect this same radiance back. The more they reflect back and reverberate their light, so much the more is the radiance of each and every one of them multiplied, or, to express it better and more aptly, the radiance is multiplied in itself and cannot be increased, for it is only one single radiance coming from one single candle, namely from the lamb of whom the Apocalypse says that he lights our heavenly city, light of living radiance, lamb of our God, our paschal candle.

Our attention should be caught upwards to invisible things, just as the paschal candle and our most sweet Christ are, for the purpose of this consideration of ours, one and the same, an inextinguishable light, true human flesh shown in one single wax, a rational soul typified in the pure wick, a single paschal candle which symbolizes our true God and the humanity which he has assumed.

In this holy city, as St. John says, neither sun nor moon are ever necessary, for the brightness of God lights it and his light is the lamb. This lamb of God is here typified in our paschal candle, which lights up the heavenly city built in the soul. The soul attains to understanding of the things of the spirit, through the created things she knows. Thus all the radiance of the crystal, the gems, the gold and the rest is from one single radiance. You can see that it is from the brightness of the candle that the gold, the crystal and gems, and the walls and towers have so much brightness, but the candle itself is just as unconsumed as it was before there were any towers or crystal or wax to which to communicate itself, for the fire of that candle is the treasure of God.

Have you understood clearly? The wall of crystal is bright virginity, which lights up the city. The different gems or precious stones are the great variety of the blessed. The twelve towers are the twelve apostles. The four shields are the four evangelists. I say in each division, four, for the four Gospels fit into each part, the holy evangelists not being more than four in number. The many golden discs or shields are the deep and solid merits of the apostolic towers, which fortify the Church and thus adorn the city. The city in its solid strength deepens the firmness of our strength. The brightness and radiance reflect back on to the gems, the gold and the rest, for thus the riches of God are inter-communicated among the blessed—from the apostle to the martyr, the martyr to the virgin, the virgin to the confessor. Each one singly would wish to give the whole to all, and all together to each one singly. He who in himself has both one and the other—I refer to the Apostle who is both martyr and confessor—does not esteem another who has only one of these titles any less, nor would that other want to have for himself the abundance of the former. The happiness of each one makes him share in all the riches of all in single charity.

We have still another tower which is a castle, a fortress, a strong dwelling, a royal house. It is the dwelling of the King, the citadel of the city, it is nearer to the candle, the very throne of God and it so far surpasses in eminence the other towers that this weak understanding of mine cannot attain to it in any measure. It is wrought by the hand of God the Father. It is the Spouse of the Son and the perfect work of God the Holy Spirit. It is established upon a very fine crystal, strong as a diamond that cannot be broken. Its wall is surrounded with a thousand precious stones and its gates are wrought of sapphire and jasper. Here it is to be noted that Sacred Scripture mentions these two precious stones or very precious gems—sapphire and jasper, for apart from their very high worth in respect of their precious quality, the one is very properly a celestial colour and the other intensely green, which signifies hope; and both have the virtue of chastity and of curing diseases of the heart and many other properties. It is said that the sapphire disposes him who wears it to reach out after God. As these conditions draw us to enter the city for which God created us, it is said that the gates of the heavenly city are of sapphire and jasper.

The gate whereby we go in to God is our magnificent Lady. Have you not read: 'I saw the gate of our Lord and God closed and no one entered through it, but Christ entered and came forth and it remained always sealed'? Its seal opened for us the gate of paradise. This tower of Sion, then, this throne of God, is our fortress, is our magnificent Lady, the universal queen of all that is not God. She is the principal tower of the royal city, much nearer to God and higher in glory. For the more precious the stone is and the greater its brightness, and the nearer it is to the candle, the more it diffuses its radiance, reflecting a much greater brightness than all the citizens, for it is much richer than any in the celestial city. All the glory it has, all its brightness, all its shimmering and all its radiance, it takes from the candle, from which all take it, while the candle remains undiminished.

This tower, this throne of God, this our royal citadel is consecrated as a church. It is certain that it is the temple of God and a sanctified city, so strong and mighty that the force of its strength is wholly in Jerusalem, as is sung of this same city. It is certain that this is the city of God of which glorious things are spoken. What thing more worthy of admiration is there that it is possible to mention than that there should be born in this city he who formed it before he was born in it, as holy David said in Psalm 86. It is true that the birth of him who formed it was within time and that he created the city before all time.

Thus in our great fortress and very great city, there is a door, through which all those who have passed have gone to enjoy God. All have entered through her, by her means and with her protection. This door is of sapphire and jasper and a most rich diamond— which are precious stones that in purity, in brightness, in value and in excellence surpass very many other stones, as they do in splendour. Therefore example is taken from them in the building of the heavenly city, founded of living stones so precious, so costly, of such great price and value that they cost the blood of the founder in the merits of Christ. There is nothing more suitable among all corporeal things with which, by way of comparison, intellectual things may be made comprehensible to corporeal men, than very precious stones. You want more light shed, but our brightness is God, Christ Jesus the blessed one, that paschal candle whose wick and wax you understand and know to be the rational soul and human flesh of our sweetest Christ, and in the essence, radiance and brightness of its light, the divine immensity—all this you embrace, and receive and have in the mystical paschal candle. Its burning brightness lights all men. Just as it is important to say that in our heavenly city there are twelve very strong towers, so it is equally important to know that there are in the city twelve gates, as is set down in the Apocalypse.

FRANCISCO ORTIZ

The dates of the birth and death of this sixteenth-century Franciscan writer are uncertain. He appears to have been born in Valladolid perhaps towards the close of the fifteenth century. After joining the Franciscan Order, he later became a noted preacher and ascetical writer. He was of Jewish descent and like many convert Jews of his time was associated in some way with the 'illuminists' or *alumbrados*. His public protest against the trial for heresy of Francisca Hernández led to his arrest and imprisonment for some years by the Inquisition. His writings were not published until after his death. The extracts here given are from the *Epístolas familiares*, almost his only work in Spanish apart from certain prayers and the *Información de la Vida Cristiana*. The *Epístolas* were first published in Zaragoza in 1552. In Latin, Francisco Ortiz left two works of importance, *De ornatu animae* (Of the adornment of the soul) and *Quadragesimale*, on Lent. Ortiz probably died in the house of his Order at Torrelaguna, where he wrote most of his works.

ON WIDOWHOOD (*Epístolas familiares*, 12)

[To Doña Catalina de Orozco, a relative. The letter speaks of the state of widowhood and of the new marriage which such people can and ought to contract with God, being espoused to him through faith.]

Most Illustrious Lady:

The grace and peace of our Lord Jesus Christ be with your ladyship and possess your whole heart, ruling all its affairs in such a way that they be pleasing to His Divine Majesty. Amen. I have received two letters from your ladyship, one by Father Alexis and the other in Zamora. Although I am late in sending a reply on paper, I can say that my soul has written your ladyship many letters, with the many desires our Lord has given me for your true consolation, lasting honour and secure prosperity. And as I feel myself urged in a new manner to desire all possible good for you, I make bold to put in writing some of the little phrases of the letters which I said my soul has written you. The first is that I have a great desire that you should truly feel in your heart that that unsearchable decree (which, as it appears to our human eyes, was in many ways

harsh and rigorous both for the illustrious Señor Hernandarias[1]—
God rest his soul—and for you and his whole household) was in
truth only a most kindly and fatherly mercy, by which God's
goodness willed to purify the very brief hour of this transitory
life for his creature, so that his creature might not perish eternally
submerged in vain prosperity and turned aside from his holy will.
Our eyes are blind when it comes to perceiving the ways of the
incomprehensible God—but this we can know, for God has
taught us so in Holy Scripture—that whom God loves he corrects
and chastises, and thus, as the prosperity of the wicked is recognized
to be a scourge, so the scourge of those who bear crosses patiently,
giving thanks to God and realizing that they deserve greater
troubles, especially if they have previously been very sinful, is a
mercy unknown to worldlings of these days, but perceived by all
those who have eyes to see and experienced by him who receives
it. In due time it will be manifested as such before the whole universe
of rational creatures, when at God's judgment-seat the truth is
known as it is and not as it is now thought to be by the world.

I should not have spoken about this matter if your ladyship had
not made some reference to it in your first letter; and because many
sheets of paper would not contain what I could say on this subject,
I will content myself with saying now that I take, and by the grace
of God will always take the same care always to offer Señor Hernandarias' soul to God, as I do in the case of my own parents, God
rest their souls. And although my prayers are poor, yet since the
sacrifice which I, though unworthy, offer each day in the Mass is of
itself exceeding rich, I trust in God's great goodness that my care
may not be profitless.

The second point is, that it is my desire that God may visit and
enlarge your ladyship's heart with such abundance of grace that,
not remembering past events, but giving increasing thanks to God
as someone who in truth owes such thanks to him, you may succeed,
the Holy Spirit being your teacher, in setting your intention much
more deeply than hitherto upon the holy state of widowhood in
which God has placed you and which your ladyship observes with
great austerity of life. To speak clearly, I mean that it would be of
great advantage to you to consider that your first and greatest
spouse is Jesus Christ, Son of the living God, everlasting King of
ages, to whom our souls promise perpetual fidelity in holy baptism.
These espousals are so real, through the great mercy of God who

---

[1] The lady's husband.

has not disdained to stoop to our lowliness, and so all-embracing, that to illustrate the sacrament of matrimony St. Paul makes the comparison of the above-mentioned espousals contracted between Christ and his Church. It is certain that holy Church does not consist of the walls alone, but of the living stones which here below are polished with tribulations that they may be worthy to be set in the heavenly building; such stones are the souls of all true and faithful Christians who are espoused to Christ in baptism. As it is certain that this heavenly Spouse lives and reigns glorious for ever, yet is absent [from us] in his bodily presence, so the souls who have contracted espousals with him, so long as they live in this exile, are called widows.

It would be a thing of great profit and spiritual joy for your ladyship if the habits and praiseworthy customs in which you persevere, in conformity with the state of life which God has given you, might be so continued outwardly with prudent moderation that the intent of your heart be enlarged within, taking all these external things as so many signs, or as a memorial of the widowhood your soul suffers and will suffer until it becomes worthy to enjoy the clear vision of Jesus Christ, your true and first and greatest spouse, sighing for his much desired presence and longing to be found worthy to enjoy him for ever.

Well do I know that there is no state in the Church which this consideration does not fit—for nuns, as a sign of this widowhood, wear a black veil, and married women run into great spiritual danger when they so give themselves up to the cares of the world that they forget they are pilgrims, leaving the truth for the shadow and losing the fruit which will remain for ever for the sake of the flower (this transitory life) which quickly fades.

But I do say this consideration is particularly applicable to widows, for their state represents the widowhood the Church suffers until the judgment day. Besides giving them superabundant interest of heavenly consolations, God overlooks in them all the blemish they incur from worldly distractions. Further, it is very true that God takes special care of them, as is shown in Holy Scripture, where he calls himself the father of orphans and judge of widows and honours them with fruit sixtyfold. Thus they have a special spiritual awareness, gratitude and careful devotion, having recourse to God, sighing for him, exercising vigilance in thinking how they can best fulfil his holy will and be prepared for the day which such persons should consider as most desirable, on which, at death, all the troubles of this painful life will cease and they will begin to enjoy the life that is real. Such was the practice of all those honourable widows praised in Holy Scripture, who were occupied day and night in fasting, prayer and works of piety.

A long business it would be for a letter if I had to write the praises of holy Judith, and of the widow of Sarepta, and of Anna the prophetess, and of her who was praised by Christ as being more generous with the two mites she gave than all the rich men offering their different gifts in the temple of God—and many others. St. Ambrose wrote a book about this. What I now long for is for God to write the above consideration on your ladyship's soul with his living finger with such art that effectively detaching your heart from earth, he will transport it to heaven; and, bringing it about that your ladyship should be content to entrust to our Lord all the children whom he has given you, that you should busy yourself in giving him thanks for the mercies received. For the sparks of holy inclinations and praiseworthy customs which God in his mercy has placed in all your children, his gifts to you, are not the first-fruits of a harvest which will be poor. Thus, amid abundance of temporal riches, God does not want his servants to love and esteem such things except for what they are; for if they were worth much, the Turk would not have so much of them, nor would God give them to his enemies, allowing his friends to suffer. True riches are better acquired by diminishing covetousness than by amassing treasures; for very often treasures are amassed to the great harm of their owner and God with great kindness removes them from those whom he is keeping for heaven. For it might chance that by clinging to them, satiated in their folly with the food of vain prosperity and blinded with the smoke of honours, such people would lose the inestimable riches and honours which have no end. Whatever is necessary for us to proceed along our way will be added, for when we seek the Kingdom of God as our first and chief care, his mercy provides as he sees fitting for us.

I do not say any more to your ladyship of Señora Doña Juana, but that I entreat our Lord always to turn on her the eyes of his mercy and fill her with the blessing of his loving kindness, and to give her what I desire for her. And although it may appear laughable folly—having delighted myself in our Lord and given him thanks for his espousals, trusting in his mercy that he will guide them with his hand for his own service and honour—to have stopped to write in this letter things which seem more suitable for nuns than for someone who has to give her attention to setting up house anew and adorning herself for weddings, yet I entreat your ladyship not to fail to glean something from what I have written if by chance you find you can profit from it; because if the house and honour and estate that our Lord will give you is to have a firm foundation and continuation and end, the first stone must be Jesus Christ our Lord, who, when he is loved and feared with one's whole heart, sustains those who cleave to him and put all their trust in him, and builds them houses of eternal bliss—far beyond these earthly dwellings which ought to be called field tents rather than houses.

I could not lightly say how much I love your ladyship in God and how faithful I am—such as I am—in recommending you to his mercy. Because the messenger for this letter is Father Alexis, I do not want to make it longer, for which reason I beg and entreat your ladyship to pardon my boldness and attribute it to the filial love it is my duty to have for you.

ST. IGNATIUS LOYOLA
(1491–1556)

The brilliant, scholarly work of Father Brodrick, S.J.,[1] and the popularization of the life of St. Ignatius by the historical novel of Louis de Wohl,[2] makes a detailed account of his life here superfluous. Let it suffice, then, to recall that he was from one of the best families of Loyola (Navarra), fought against the French at Pamplona, was shot in the leg and, during his enforced and prolonged convalescence, in default of other literature was forced to content himself with reading the lives of the saints. This brought about his conversion. Henceforth he thought only of giving himself to God and saving souls. After a pilgrimage to Jerusalem, he set about the business of his education, going first to the then newly founded university of Alcalá de Henares and afterwards to Paris. The Society of Jesus, his life's work, was founded in 1540.

The 'Spiritual Exercises', by which St. Ignatius is, perhaps, chiefly known, owe much to García de Cisneros[3] and something, perhaps, to Ludolph the Carthusian's 'Life of Christ'. The working out of them is St. Ignatius' own. He founded the Society, formed its first members and then gave them what was to be both their charter and their instrument, the 'Exercises'. They are so well known that only the briefest extract is given here, the other passage reproduced being from St. Ignatius' 'Letters'.

MEDITATIONS THAT WEARY AND OTHERS THAT
DELIGHT THE SOUL AND IN WHICH THE BODY
FINDS REST; REASONS WHY CERTAIN MEDITATIONS
ARE INJURIOUS TO HEALTH; ADVANTAGES OF A
HEALTHY BODY—FOR SO LONG AS IT IS FIRM IN THE
LOVE OF GOD, THE SOUL DOES NOT SHRINK FROM NOR
FEAR TOO MUCH THE TEMPTATIONS AND INVOLUNTARY
WEAKNESSES SHE SEES IN HERSELF.
(Letter 8, to Sister Teresa Rejadella)

The grace and love of Christ our Lord be always our help and our protection.

I have received two letters of yours on different occasions; to

1 J. Brodrick, S. J.: *Origins of the Jesuits* and *Progress of the Jesuits*, London, 1940 and 1947; *St. Ignatius Loyola*, 1956.
2 Louis de Wohl: *The Golden Thread*, London, 1953.
3 See p. 1.

the first it seems to me I replied at length, and you should already have received it. In the second you say the same as in the first, except for a few remarks, and to those only I shall briefly reply.

You say that you find in yourself so much ignorance and too much preoccupation with trifles[1] (and it is a great deal to recognize this), and that it seems to you that this is aggravated by many people expressing their opinions, few of which are put into action. I agree with what you say, that he who resolves little, understands little and helps less. But the Lord, who sees this, brings good from it.

Every meditation in which the understanding works fatigues the body. Other meditations, orderly but unfatiguing, which quieten the understanding and do not exercise the inner core of the mind, but which are pursued without any strain whether interior or external—such do not weary the body but rest it, except perhaps in two respects, of which the first is in depriving you of the natural sustenance and recreation you have to give the body. I use the term 'sustenance' when someone through busying himself in such meditations, does not remember to give the body its natural refreshment, going beyond the proper hours. By the term 'recreation' I mean, of course, devout recreation, leaving the mind to wander where it will among good or indifferent things, so long as they are not evil. The second is what happens to many persons given to prayer and contemplation. When they retire to rest, through having made much use of the understanding they cannot afterwards sleep, for then they think of the things contemplated and imagined, into which the enemy then makes much attempt to introduce good things so that the body may suffer through lack of sleep—a thing to be utterly avoided. When the body is healthy, you can do much; when it is sick I do not know what you can do. A healthy body is a considerable help in the doing of much evil and of much good—much evil in those who have a depraved will and bad habits; much good in those who have their will fixed on God our Lord and set in the way of good habits.

If I did not know what those meditations or exercises of yours are and how much time they take, and, besides, what Cáceres told you, I should not be able to write to you in detail. Here I repeat once again that, before all else, you should think that your Lord loves you (which is certainly the case) and that you ought to respond to him with the same love, not troubling about evil, unchaste or

<hr>

[1] *poquedades.*

sensual thoughts, nor bothering about trifles or lukewarmness, when they are involuntary. For all that, or part of it, neither St. Peter nor St. Paul succeeded in driving away; but much can be achieved, though not all, with paying no attention to any of it. For just as I have not to be saved through the good works of the good angels, so I have not to be condemned for the bad thoughts and weaknesses which the bad angels, the world and the flesh put before me. All that God our Lord wants is that my soul should be conformed to his divine Majesty. The soul when it is thus conformed makes the body (whether it will or no) move in conformity with the divine will. In achieving this conformity consists our greatest struggle and the pleasure of God's eternal and highest Goodness.

May he, through his infinite loving-kindness and grace, deign always to take us by the hand.

Venice, *September* 11th, 1536

THE END OF MAN
(from 'The Spiritual Exercises')

Man has been created to praise, reverence and serve God our Lord, and by this means to save his soul: and the other things upon the face of the earth are created for man, and to help him in the prosecution of the end for which he is created. Whence it follows that man has to use such things just in so far as they help him towards his end; and he should avoid them in so far as they hinder him in that respect. For this reason it is necessary that we should be indifferent to all created things in everything that is within the sphere of our free will and is not forbidden to it, so that for our part we do not desire health more than sickness, riches more than poverty, honour than dishonour, a long life rather than a short one, and similarly in all the rest; only desiring and choosing that which leads us more surely to the end for which we were created.

FRANCISCO DE OSUNA
(*c.* 1497–1542)

Francisco de Osuna was born at the close of the fifteenth century (probably in the year 1497), at the town whose name he bears, Osuna, in the province of Seville, where his parents were in the service of Count Juan Téllez Girón. When quite a child he was taken by his father and mother to Africa and witnessed the taking of Tripoli by the Spaniards in 1510.

He entered the Franciscan Order early, pursuing his studies in the university of Salamanca. During these years at the university, despite the fact that he was then, as always, delicate in health, Francisco, while never neglecting his studies, devoted himself with all the intensity of his being to prayer and contemplation. At the age of twenty-eight he wrote his famous *Abecedario*, or 'Alphabet', the treatise on the spiritual life which so greatly helped St. Teresa and which was first printed in Toledo in 1527.

Francisco did not spend all his life in one place. We hear of him making the pilgrimage to Santiago de Compostela and also attending chapters of his Order in Paris and Toulouse. Later he spent some time in the Low Countries, where he superintended the publication of his works in Latin; but the cold, damp climate of Flanders increased the sufferings of his already delicate body, and when he was elected General Commissary of the Franciscan Order for the Indies, he had to exercise his office by proxy, owing to the poor state of his health.

Francisco died in April 1542. The place and circumstances of his death are unknown.

The *Abecedarios* are six in number. The first treats of the circumstances of the Passion. The second is a work on asceticism. The third Alphabet, the one which so greatly influenced St. Teresa, is concerned with prayer and the contemplative life. The fourth Alphabet treats of love, the fifth of poverty and riches, and the sixth of Christ's Wounds. The 'Third Spiritual Alphabet' was translated into English by a Benedictine of Stanbrook in 1931. The 'alphabet' form of treating a subject was popular in the fifteenth and early sixteenth centuries. It was a feature of Hebrew writing and is familiar to us from the arrangement of the Lamentations of Jeremias.

HOW THE ANGELS WEPT AT THE PASSION OF CHRIST
(from the 'First Spiritual Alphabet')

... It is, however, to be noted that the text mentions two kinds of handmaids who wept with the daughter of Jephte,[1] namely, members of the household and companions. The members of the household, that is souls that are holy, have already been spoken of. The companions who are almost equals of the King's daughter, for they are admitted to share the same table, represent the angelic hosts who are said to sit down at table with Christ in his Sacred Humanity, for like the Sacred Humanity they can see God, though not so closely.

The most precious soul of Christ found consolation in these angelic hosts and in his own way called them to mourn with him on the celestial mountains—all the angelic hosts cried with Christ to the Eternal Father, 'Father, if the thing is possible (all justice and the divine plan having been safeguarded), may this terrible chalice of the most grievous Passion pass from me.' And it is clear that the angels took part in this, for when Christ was in mortal agony in the anticipated presence of death (as the Evangelist tells us),[2] there appeared to him an angel from heaven strengthening him.

That the angels wept and mourned with Christ as far as they could, St. Augustine shows, saying: 'Oh what a thing of grief beyond measure it was to see the Son of God die. Which of the angels or archangels there could refrain from weeping, when against every order of nature, immortal God was stripped and shown like a man.' Nor should it astonish anyone that the angels should show feeling in this way, for just as it was possible for God to die in respect of the flesh and humanity which he received as true man, so it was possible for the good angels to weep and feel sorrow at the death and passion of their Lord, taking and forming bodies from the air in order to weep. For in Holy Scripture we find many angels who have taken bodies to do things which were not in accordance with their spiritual nature. How much more, then, should the angels take bodies to show grief and compassion at the death of our Lord. That which Isaias prophesied when he said 'The angels of peace shall weep bitterly'[3] was fulfilled.

[1] Cf. Judges 11.   [2] Luke 22.
[3] Isaias 33:7 [D].

OF THE SLEEP OF CHRIST ON THE CROSS
(from the 'First Spiritual Alphabet')

... When people of rank go on pilgrimage or to war, they carry
with them a bed, and the Son of God when he came down from
heaven, likewise took as his bed Calvary and the cross, of which
the same Lord says: 'In the darkness appears my bed.' Hard and
narrow was the cross indeed, an uneasy bed; especially when, as
the Evangelist says, there was darkness over the whole earth,
because the King of glory was sleeping the sleep of death. For at
the time of sleep they close the windows and put out the tapers
and set someone to guard the body of the king. The chief windows
through which light enters the house of this world are the sun and
the moon which bring us light from the other life, and the tapers
are the stars which give light at night. All these ceased to give light
that our Redeemer might sleep in darkness on his bed. The guards
were the centurion and his men who were guarding our Lord on
the cross, for no one showed him mercy nor did him any kindness.
Wherefore, as Origen says, the Romans were wont to break the
legs of those crucified without delay so that they might not suffer
so much, but as Pilate had determined, in accordance with the
sentence he gave, to torture Christ as much as the good pleasure
of his accusers demanded, he wanted to allow him to suffer more.
For this he set guards at the cross, and did not allow them to break
his legs forthwith. Christ our Lord, however, seeing that they were
prolonging his death, cried to his Father asking why he had left
him in the hands of his enemies. After his cry he said that all was
finished that he had to suffer in the flesh, and therefore, since the
work of our redemption was completed, of his own will he sent
forth his spirit to the Father from this bed. The centurion was
dumbfounded at seeing the Lord die when he willed to do so.
He realized that he was truly the Son of God through seeing
him die completely of his own free will, and with so marvellous a
death.

We ought then to have the cross and passion much in mind. Let
us draw near to the bed of our father and Lord on which he lay ill
with grief for our sins and on which being nigh to death he made
his will and very great bequests even to the thieves, to the point
of granting them heaven. . . .

ON THE GIVING OF THANKS
(from the 'Third Spiritual Alphabet')

The giving of thanks to those who confer favours upon us is a thing of such excellence and goodness that if we consider the matter we shall find this virtue naturally implanted in almost all creatures. For even if they cannot speak, by their deeds they show more gratitude to their benefactors than men do by word, for we see that the earth, visited by heaven with rain and fine weather, immediately, as if to render thanks, begins to bud forth and send up its plants and flowers towards heaven in return for what it has received. Again, because the gardener bestows care upon growing the young trees, they, even when they have grown to their full height, bend down their fruit so that he can gather it and as it were say by their action, 'Take this fruit in return for the kindness you do us in taking care of us.' Moreover when the sun comes out, we see the little birds chirping and singing. Who can doubt that they do so in gratitude because the sun comes to give them warmth and light, delivering them from the cold and danger of the night? All the rivers run swiftly to the sea to thank it for producing them; they return to the hands whence they came, giving thanks because they have been sent forth.

It would take too long to relate how grateful many of the animals are. Their gratitude and thanks are so remarkable that those who have written about it are scarcely believed. The reason for not believing the great gratitude of the animals, it seems to me, is the little of it we have ourselves. This is quite apparent, for we do not appreciate our good until we have lost it and this comes through not having given sufficient thanks to those who give us the good things, so that our benefactors have to wait to be thanked until we lose their benefits. Then, with the lack of them, we realize what we have enjoyed in the past and are moved to give thanks.

It is certainly a great evil that the lack of a thing should move us more than the thing itself; the desire of possessing makes us forget him who made us possessors. On account of this evil propensity which we mortals have, I cannot find anyone to whom we can be better and more rightly compared than to the pigs who, standing under the oak tree, enjoy the acorns, but never lift their heads to see where they come from, nor do they bother to know, as if it did not concern them.

THAT SILENCE IS GOOD
(from the 'Third Spiritual Alphabet')

The next point under this Letter counsels you to be spiritually deaf, for, as our Lord says, because the first man listened to the voice of his wife, many evils came to him. Our wife is our sensuality which reason must in no way listen to or argue with. The fact that Abraham was commanded to listen to the voice of Sara does not in any way contradict this, for that was when Sara had grown old, as the Scripture says.[1] So our sensuality is quietened down when it is well under the control of reason. What it tells us when it has become reasonable is that we should cast out the bond woman and her son, thrusting aside the imaginations and distractions which arise from nature, in order that we may thus be alone without the sound of any voice, for nature thunders at our soul like a mill which never ceases making a harmful din. Such din must not be found in the house of God when it is built, for there there must be heard no sound of hammer, nor saw, nor tool of iron, for all these sounds are harsh and do not soothe the soul.

This third point shows that we should also be inwardly dumb, not uttering any word—even be it sublime, as the mother of Samuel advises (in the book of Exodus).[2] For the Lord is God of all knowledge and he is better pleased that we should listen to him in silence and in spirit and in truth, rather than speak to him with words. The greater the silence with which we entreat him, the more favourably he listens and grants what we ask him. This we see from the example of Moses who, although he uttered no word, because he prayed in silence received an answer as if he had been importuning the Lord, who said, 'Why are you crying loudly to me?' That the Lord grants what they desire to those who are silent is also clear from Zachary who, when he was dumb, begot St. John the Baptist whose name means grace. He did not speak until St. John was born and afterwards he spoke much better than before for he had become the glorious prophet whom we know.[3] If we want to engender the Lord's grace in our souls by means of his favour, and to know how to speak gloriously of heavenly things, first, as Gerson says, we have to keep silence even in our inmost hearts, according to what Jeremias wrote: 'The Lord is

---

[1] Genesis 21.
[2] Not, of course, the book of Exodus; actually I Kings 2:3.
[3] i.e. by uttering the *Benedictus*.

good to them that wait upon him, to the soul who seeks him.' To
show us how we have to seek him, he then says: 'It is good to wait
with silence for the salvation of God';[1] and to show how continu-
ously we ought to be in this state he adds: 'It is good for a man when
he has borne the yoke from his youth.' 'He shall sit down as a
solitary and hold his peace: because he hath taken it upon himself.'[2]
All these sayings warn us that we should be silent in our heart and
keep there perpetual quiet if we want to rise to high contemplation.
Wherefore in respect of that saying the gloss says: Wait with
silence. This prophet took such advantage of this that, excluding
and shutting out all things there are in the world, he passed beyond
the dignity of the angels, to be able to find him whom he loved.
This, he declares, is to be hoped for as the highest good. For the
sake of being always united and linked to God, he says that it is
good for a man to bear the yoke from his youth. This yoke is to
be solitary and sit and be quiet. This is what the gloss says.

We should also know that naturally the world is deaf. By this
we are to understand in this case that he who is inwardly dumb,
not forming any thought within himself, must also be deaf, not
admitting those many thoughts which, as the Wise Man said, weary
the earthly habitation, weighing it down and repressing it. For this
reason, advisedly, there were included under our Letter these two
words 'dumb' and 'deaf', so that by the one the thought that we
produce and think deliberately is forbidden to us, and by the other,
that which arises through the much business and vanity in which
we are engaged. On these two points St. Bonaventure says, commenting on the 'Mystical Theology' of St. Dionysius, that because
this apprehending is of things above and not of things below, we
are commanded to set aside the exterior senses. This, according to
St. Bonaventure, is not only to be understood of the functioning
of the senses from without, but also from within. The working or
experimental knowledge of it comes from the hand of God, who
says he has given to the recollected soul rings in the ears that she
may be deaf to vain thoughts; and also rings upon her mouth, so
that she may not form or cause them within herself.[3]

These three words, 'blind', 'deaf' and 'dumb', can also be
applied to the three powers of our soul. The understanding should
be blind in the way we have said, not using knowledge which can
destroy this suspension. The will must be deaf to the love to which

---

[1] Lamentations 3:25, 26 [D].
[2] *Ibid.*, 28 [D].   [3] Cf. Ezechiel 19.

creatures invite it. Speaking of these two things St. Bonaventure says: One should first leave the consideration of and affection for sensible things, and then the contemplation of all intelligible things; so that pure love may reign supreme. The memory must be dumb, not handling or turning over anything capable of expression, so that Jesus may enter, although not according to the flesh but to the spirit, when these three doors are closed, as he came among his disciples after the Resurrection. For the doors of the Cenacle, which is a figure of the soul where God comes in to sup if we will only open to him the door of consent, were closed. . . .

OF THE THREE MANNERS OF SILENCE
(from the 'Third Spiritual Alphabet')

There are in recollection three ways of being quiet or three manners of silence, leaving aside the others which are not to the point here. The first is when all fantasies and imaginations and likenesses of visible things cease in the soul, which is thus silent to all created things. This was what holy Job desired when he said: 'For now I should have been asleep and still; and should have rest in my sleep with kings and consuls of the earth, who build themselves solitudes.'[1] According to St. Gregory, we are asleep to temporal things and silent within ourselves, when within, in the most hidden recess of our soul, we withdraw to the contemplation of the Creator. The saints, who are here called kings and consuls, build themselves solitudes when they desire nothing of this world. Neither are they disturbed in heart through any tumult of unruly desires, but cast aside all unlawful movements from their heart with the right hand of holy reasoning, despising all transitory things and the extravagant thoughts which arise from them. And as they desire only an eternal dwelling place and love nothing of this world, such people enjoy great peace of soul.

The second kind of silence to be found in recollection occurs when the soul, completely quiet, finds in itself a kind of spiritual idleness, feeling that it is with Mary at the feet of our Lord and saying: 'I will hear what the Lord God shall speak concerning me.' The Lord replies: 'Hearken, O daughter, and see, and incline thine ear and forget thy people and thy father's house.' This second manner of silence is well compared to hearing, for not only is the listener silent, but he also desires that all else may be silent in his

[1] Job 3:13, 14 [D].

presence, in order that his whole attention may be turned to him who is speaking to him, especially when he does not know where the speaker is as in the present case. For, as it is said in the Gospel, we hear the voice of God—that is, his inspiration—we do not know where it goes nor whence it comes. For this reason we should be very quiet and listen very intently.

Thus we have two kinds of silence, the one stilling in ourselves the imagination and thoughts which flit about in our memory; the other a forgetfulness of ourselves with the conversion of the whole of the inward man to God alone. The first silence is of outward things in us, the second a blessed peace in which we are silent to our very selves and in which we turn to God with a response of receptive submission. This is shown in the sacred animals of Ezechiel[1] of which it is said: 'For when a voice came from above the firmament, that was over their heads, they stood and let down their wings.' According to what we have said, the voice is the divine inspiration which is received in the ear of the soul without any expression of words, but solely with the presence of God which allows itself to be felt. For this [reason] Job[2] says that secretly and silently he heard the hidden word that was spoken to him and he received the strains and echoes of its faint sound. This inspired voice is above the firmament which is the highest part of reason, being joined immediately to God by love. Of the sacred winged creatures, who are contemplatives, it is said that they are then standing, because when this voice is heard in the soul, it rises to high things, remaining suspended as if transported into God, like the apostles when they saw Christ going up to heaven. Thus Ezechiel was ordered to stand upon his feet that God might speak to him,[3] for, as St. Gregory says, the standing upon one's feet is silent worship which makes us cling to God as Job[4] clung to him in his soul. This means that all operation of the powers of the soul almost ceases in order that, as it diminishes, the soul may receive Wisdom.

To let down the wings is to apply one's highest power to receive the divine inflow which is pouring itself into the soul. In this, as the gloss says, contemplatives hold their strength as nothing, but apply themselves to God, being silent in order that, failing in themselves, they may find themselves in him, as in that which they desire. 'My soul refused to be comforted. I remembered God and was delighted and was exercised and my spirit swooned away.'[5]

---

1 Ezechiel 1:22–24 [D].
2 Actually Eliphaz the Themanite, cf. Job 12:4.
3 Ezechiel 2:1.   4 i.e. Eliphaz.   5 Psalm 75:3 [D].

The third kind of silence within the understanding takes place in God, when the whole soul is transformed into him and tastes abundantly of his sweetness, and in this the soul sleeps as in a cellar of wine. It sleeps not desiring anything more, for it finds itself satisfied. It sleeps even in itself, forgetting the weakness of its condition, through seeing itself so divinized and united to its source and clothed with his brightness, like another Moses after having entered into the cloud that was upon the summit of the mountain. This in a true manner happened to St. John when after the Last Supper he leaned upon the breast of the Lord. Then all his senses were silent.

It may happen in this third kind of silence that the understanding is silent and captive, or rather occupied, so that it hears nothing of what is said to it, nor does it exercise its judgment on anything that passes close to it, for it does not even advert to or hear it. In regard to this, an old man whose confession I used to hear told me in great secrecy—he had spent more than fifty years in such things—that among other mysterious things which had happened to him, was the fact that he listened to certain words and things about God without understanding a word; so silent and occupied was his mind within that no created thing could take shape in him. I told him that then he ought to have withdrawn into solitude. To this he replied that the voices were to him like organ tones, in which his soul took pleasure whenever he heard them, and which as it were acted as a counterpoint to praise the Lord in a manner which could be felt though he could not explain it.

This Letter does not say that you should quieten your intelligence but your understanding, for as Richard[1] says, comprehension of invisible things belongs to pure intelligence. He says that the intelligence is pure when the understanding is centred upon some sublime truth without any admixture of the imagination. But to attain to this it is necessary, as the same writer says, that you should learn to gather together the 'remnants of Israel', that is, your understanding, quietening it; and that you should study to restrain the wanderings of memory and accustom yourself to dwell intimately within yourself forgetting all things without, if you are striving after the contemplation of heavenly things and sigh for the experimental knowledge of what is divine. According to this doctor, the intelligence does not see the invisible things of God as reason sees them, for reason, investigating and arguing through

1 i.e. Richard of St. Victor.

effects and causes, comes to know things which are hidden and absent as if it actually saw them. Not in this manner, but as we are wont to see material things with visible, corporeal sight and in their actual presence, so does pure intelligence perceive invisibly things which are invisible and makes contact with spiritual things in their presence and their essence, knowing that they are not bound or confined within outward appearances. So that when man ceases to attend to the imagination which revolves around visible things, or to reason which is wont to go arguing from one corporeal thing to another to investigate the spiritual—but represents God before him as a most pure spirit, divested of all things that have appearances, and rests in that pure veneration without his attention wandering to any other thing, then it can be said that he is using his intelligence.

ST. PETER OF ALCÁNTARA
(1499-1562)

A dark, lean man, almost twisted crooked with austerities, wearing a ragged brown habit dragging in the dust, tramping the roads on foot and satisfied with a hunk of bread every other day or so—such were the marks by which men recognized St. Peter of Alcántara.[1] Poverty, detachment, unworldliness.

He was born at Alcántara in Extremadura in 1499, his father being governor of the city. He early showed an attraction both for the contemplative life and for austerity and, after studying law in the university of Salamanca, joined the Franciscan Reform. He was sixteen—university studies began early in those days. In 1524 he was ordained and soon acquired a reputation as a preacher. For the most part his ministry was exercised around Plasencia and Badajoz, not far from the frontiers of Portugal.

In 1538 St. Peter was elected Provincial of Extremadura. In a Chapter at Plasencia he drew up Constitutions for the province, but this alienated his brethren. In 1541, free now from the cares of office, he withdrew to Portugal where, with another friar, he embraced a life that was almost eremitical. In 1544 he returned to Spain and, nine years later, withdrew into complete retirement. In 1555 he obtained permission from Pope Julius III to found houses where Franciscan life as he conceived it should be lived to the full—a venture which was to be under the jurisdiction of the Conventuals. He established two houses of his reform—Pedroso and Plasencia. His movement absorbed certain other houses of the Order and was organized in 1561 as the Province of St. Joseph. His friars were known as the *Fratres Conventuales Reformati*. In 1563 they were placed under the jurisdiction of the Observants. Their churches, monasteries and cells were all on a very modest scale. They practised perpetual abstinence and the brethren went barefoot without even sandals. No libraries were allowed, only a few books in each cell for the use of its occupant.

As is well known, St. Peter of Alcántara was a great friend and counsellor of St. Teresa. She first met him only a few years before his death. Being troubled with uncertainty as to whether her ways of prayer were right, she obtained permission from the Convent of the Incarnation to stay with her friend, Doña Guiomar de Ulloa, that she might be able to talk with St. Peter and have the benefit of his advice. She regarded both his personal help and his writings as of the highest importance. The

---

[1] Cf. Marcelle Auclair, *St. Teresa of Ávila*, p. 103 (London, 1952).

saint several times appeared to her after his death, helping her with his counsel.

St. Peter was great as preacher, spiritual writer, director of souls. He was also a good organizer. Although his personal life was extremely austere, he was pleasant and approachable in manner and his counsels were always prudent and wise. He died at Arenas, near Oropesa, on St. Luke's Day, 1562, at the age of sixty-three.

The 'Treatise on Prayer and Meditation' from which the present extract is taken was written probably in 1533 when the saint was Guardian of the isolated monastery of San Onofre de Lapa, at the request of Don Rodrigo de Chaves and his wife, Doña Francisca, of the noble families of Plasencia.[1] Near to and depending on Lapa were four hermitages, one of which, dedicated to Saint John the Baptist, was constructed at the expense of Jane Dormer who had married the Conde Duque Gomez Suarez de Figuera, first Duke of Feria. The Duke and his English wife were accustomed to spend Lent there.

The treatise mentioned is practically the only one of the saint's writings which has come down to us.[2] The others (well known to St. Teresa), or some of them, may well exist in manuscript in some of the as yet un-catalogued libraries in Spain. As St. Peter himself tells us, the 'Treatise' is a compilation. He also adds that it is intended for simple folk. The book is clearly based on a work on prayer by Luis de Granada, but an adaptation for certain purposes and for certain classes of readers may have its uses and the 'Treatise' may thus claim to have an independent *raison d'être*. In any event the outlook on such matters in the sixteenth century was vastly different from that of today, since men then wrote not to enhance their own reputation but to make known something that was good. Moreover St. Peter acknowledges his indebtedness in a preface to his own treatise, while Luis de Granada never made the slightest protest.

OF TEN THINGS WHICH HINDER DEVOTION
(from 'Treatise on Prayer and Meditation', ch. 3)

Just as there are things which help devotion, so also are there things which hinder it, among which the first is our sins, not only the mortal but also the venial ones, for the latter, although they do not take away charity, take away the fervour of charity, which is the same as devotion, and therefore they should be avoided with all care, if not for the harm they do, at least for the great good which they prevent.

Another hindrance is the remorse of conscience which proceeds

[1] Don Rodrigo gave the saint a house at Pedroso, not far from Ciudad Rodrigo. He founded a friary there.

[2] A copy of the 'Rule of Life for Persons of Quality living in the World' is extant in the British Museum.

from these very sins (when it is excessive), for it makes the soul restless and cast down, faint and weak for every good practice.

Scruples also hinder devotion for the same reason, for they are like thorns, which prick and disturb the conscience and do not allow it to rest and repose in God and enjoy true peace.

Another hindrance is a certain bitterness and despondency of heart and inordinate sadness, for with this the joy and sweetness of a good conscience and spiritual gladness is very ill matched.

Too many cares constitute another hindrance. They are those mosquitoes from Egypt which disturb the soul and do not allow it to sleep the spiritual sleep which lulls the soul in prayer, nay, more than that, they disturb and turn it aside from its spiritual exercise.

Another hindrance is found in gifts and sensual comforts (when a man is too much taken up with them), for he who gives himself up in considerable measure to the consolations of the world does not deserve those of the Holy Spirit, as St. Bernard says.[1]

Too many occupations are likewise a hindrance, for they take up one's time and submerge the spirit, and thus leave a man without time or heart to attend to God.

Delight in too much eating and drinking likewise hinders, and especially prolonged suppers, for these make a very bad bed for spiritual exercises and for holy vigils, for when the body is heavy and full of nourishment, the soul is but poorly equipped for taking flight to higher things.

A further hindrance is the vice of curiosity, whether of the senses or of the understanding, which consists in wanting to hear and see and know many things and to desire things which are exquisite, curious and finely made. All this takes up time, entangles the senses, disturbs the soul, dividing it into many parts, and this impedes devotion.

Lastly, the interruption of all those holy exercises hinders devotion, unless they are omitted for the sake of some devout or just necessity, for the spirit of devotion is very delicate, and once it has gone it does not return, or only with much difficulty. And for this, just as the trees, and human bodies, need their normal food and drink and die and wither for the lack of it, so is it with devotion when it lacks [spiritual] food and drink.

All this has been said here briefly, in order that the memory may more easily retain this description of those things which anyone who wants to do so, may verify with practice and long experience.

1 Serm. 5 in Natali. Dom.

BD. ALONSO DE OROZCO
(1500–1591)

Alonso de Orozco was born at Oropesa in the province of Toledo. As a child, having first served from the age of eight in the cathedral at Talavera de la Reina, he became a *seise*[1] in Toledo cathedral where he was taught music and completed his education. At fourteen he entered the university at Salamanca, studying there for eight years. He then joined the Augustinian Order, making profession at Salamanca at the hands of St. Thomas of Villanueva, as did also one of his brothers.

Alonso—who was beatified by Pope Leo XIII in 1882—was a man of most holy life whose only personal ambition was to remain hidden in God. He was austere and mortified, sleeping only three hours and taking but one poor meal each day, and gave himself, as far as was possible, to uninterrupted prayer. In 1530, at Granada, he had a severe illness. He also had to bear for many years the trial of scruples.

Alonso had a great desire to go to the Indies as a missionary, but ill-health obliged him to remain in Spain. Between 1538 and 1546, despite his love of the hidden life, he was called to rule over various houses of his Order, being prior successively of Soria, Medina del Campo, Sevilla and Granada, and in 1551 he was named prior of Valladolid. Afterwards he was transferred to Madrid, where he came under the notice of Philip II, who, many years later, visited him in his last illness. In Madrid Alonso was greatly revered by all for his sanctity. Even in extreme old age, he never failed to be present at midnight Matins. Each day after Mass he would visit the sick in his monastery and bring them delicacies. With the alms he received from King Philip, he helped foreigners.

In 1542, at Seville, our Lady appeared to Bd. Alonso of Orozco in dreams, saying the one word: 'Write'. From that moment he gave his pen no rest. He is ranked among the great writers of the Golden Age. He wrote many works of spirituality, one of the best known of which is 'The Mount of Contemplation', from which the present extract is taken. It is in the form of a dialogue between Orozco himself and a less experienced Augustinian friar whom he was instructing in the ways of contemplation. Bd. Orozco also gave us a 'Chronicle of the Order of St. Augustine', and his 'Confessions'—invaluable as biographical material.

[1] A choir boy who takes part in the sacred dances.

WHAT CONTEMPLATION IS AND THE THINGS
WHICH FAVOUR IT
(ch. 7 of 'The Mount of Contemplation')

 OROSIUS: Whoever goes up to the mount of the Lord to contemplate his majesty, Augustine, will receive blessing and mercy
from his Saviour.

AUGUSTINE: See, brother, what wonderful treasures the Saviour
of the world has in store for those who wish to serve him with a
pure heart and true desire and who are resolute in their will to go
forth to the heavenly fields and forests where Jesus Christ our God
and most precious treasure was hidden and enclosed in a sepulchre,
whence he rose glorious to ascend up to heaven and be seated at
the right hand of the Father. More generous by far than the
patriarch Isaac blessing his son Jacob, the Father gives his blessing
not in word but in deed, giving to the souls who contemplate him
of the dew of heaven and the abundance of earth. Contemplation
is well termed heavenly dew, for it is a sovereign gift and no human
strength can merit it. This is the precious ointment which holy
David says comes down from Christ's head to his beard[1]: namely
the holy and righteous men who, despising all visible things, were
yet lords of the whole earth. And from the beard it comes down
to the garments, that the virtues of the soul, which are the garments
with which it is clothed, may gather strength and give off a fragrant
odour. And since the fountain whence sweetness and delight in
contemplation arise is Christ, the prophet David most truly says
here that it is blessing and mercy that we receive from our God.

Thus if we want to consider what contemplation is, we shall
say that it is a free, clear act of the understanding with a view to
getting to know the highest truth, that is, our God, in himself or
in his creatures. The contemplation we are discussing here is quite
different from that which Aristotle spoke of in his 'Ethics', for the
philosophers were satisfied with merely understanding the divine
perfections and were not concerned about loving God or about the
humble giving of thanks to the Lord of the world from whom they
were receiving such great mercies. For this reason St. Paul says
that their presumption miserably overthrew them. The contemplation of the Christian must be rooted in humility and accompanied
by perfect love, because not only does the mind soar to high things,
but love and its effects rise with it.

[1] Psalm 132.

OROSIUS: How can you call contemplation, as you have done, a free, clear consideration, when in this life we are not allowed to know God except by faith?

AUGUSTINE: It is quite true, brother, that in comparison with the contemplation which the blessed angels have in heaven, your earthly contemplation must be called imperfect, and it was for this reason that St. Paul said that in this life we see as in a glass and in figure—he means that our contemplation is by faith rising from these visible things to the invisible things of God, as in the case of a man who comes to know the cause through its effects. Afterwards it will be perfect contemplation, seeing God in clear vision, God who ordained that our bliss and happiness should in some sort begin here by the contemplation of his grandeurs, and should come to perfect fruition in heaven. This is what our father St. Augustine says—that contemplation is promised us in heaven as the final end of our works.

OROSIUS: Since, then, we are now at the gate of the garden where the king of glory was crucified, guide me into it, for I greatly desire to receive his blessing and his mercies which are promised me.

AUGUSTINE: We have three gates to pass through before we enter within, brother, for, like Queen Esther, we must proceed in an orderly way if we are to come to contemplate King Assuerus, Jesus Christ our God, seated on the throne of his majesty which is his holy cross. The first gate through which we have to pass to contemplation is holy reading. The second is unceasing meditation. The third is fervent prayer—to which contemplation is closely allied.

Our father St. Augustine, in the book he wrote on the heavenly ladder,[1] sets out these four things with great genius and subtlety. To reading he gave the function of seeking the treasure. Meditation, he said, will find it, prayer digs for it with all its might, and contemplation sets it forth in clear light. The holy doctor bases this on those words of the Gospel: 'Seek and ye shall find—knock and it shall be opened to you.' So that seeking God is the part of holy reading, just as worldly reading, which is the promoter of vice and destroyer of virtue, leads to losing him. As you well know, brother, when our Lord's most holy Mother and Joseph were seeking the child Jesus, St. Luke says that they found him in the temple among the doctors. If, then, you want to find this Lord of mercy, read

[1] *De scala paradisae.*

learned and spiritual doctors, for St. Lipsianus[1] says: 'As in prayer
we speak with God, in reading our God speaks to us.' Origen
extols holy reading to such an extent that he says it is another
heaven of delight. Thither God bears away the souls of every one
of us, as he bore Adam away to the earthly paradise—that through
what we read we may taste the different fruits of the virtues and may
exercise ourselves in perfect works.

OROSIUS: Many Christians stray far out of the way, for they
waste time in idle reading. The way they are following is clear, for
the profit they derive from it is vain and worldly thoughts, a zeal
which lacks simplicity and eagerness for malice—and to this end
is their endeavour and practice directed. This is clear [both] in
their countenance and from their disjointed life. May our God
remedy this, for it is a great pity that such bad books should be so
freely bought and sold—it would be better to call them fire or
brands from hell than reading for Christians, for they kindle the
vices and evil inclinations of men. I shall be most happy to learn
from you what books should be read and what counsel should be
followed in reading.

AUGUSTINE: We owe much to those who in what they wrote
enlightened our understanding, and with cogent reasoning praised
the virtues and reproved the vices, but the book which not only
speaks to the understanding but also awakens the will to the love
of God should be held in high esteem. Hardly ever should we allow
it to leave our hands, and it should be read with the mind in repose,
doing violence to oneself to pay attention, and casting aside every
other thought. Do not go jumping about from one book to another,
nor begin by reading the end. For, as a philosopher said, we enjoy
variety in what we read, but perseverance in reading is what
brings us profit. You should always pick out certain passages from
what you have read and fix them in your mind. For although the
remembrance of them be but the matter of an hour, they are of great
profit for the soul. He who has eaten well profits little if on rising
from table he then turns to seek for food again. Similarly, he who
has read of high things and, closing the book, remembers nothing,
will profit little. I say little; I do not say there is no profit at all,
for however it be done, the soul draws some strength from reading.
Always have a definite time each day for reading, just as you should
have for prayer and contemplation.

Now as you see that after this first gate it is necessary to pass to

---

[1] I have been unable to trace this reference.

the second, which is meditation, you should know that just as reading gives the food of doctrine into our hand, by meditation what we read is broken up in the mouth and digested. In this respect, you should know that there is a great difference between mere thinking, and meditating, for 'cogitation' is in the imaginative faculty which is never at rest but goes wandering from one side to the other—but meditation is in the understanding whose function it is to consider perseveringly the nature, order and conditions of a thing.

OROSIUS: As these things are so indispensable[1] and yet are hidden, for they take place in the soul, they seem difficult to understand—give me some simile so that they become clearer.

AUGUSTINE: I will give you a very clear comparison which our father St. Augustine puts forward in the place we are speaking of. When I read in the Gospel: Blessed are the pure in heart for they shall see God—then my mind begins to meditate and consider where this purity can have become lost and the heart stained, and finding it to be clear that all the harm comes from the senses being ill guarded, in particular one's hearing, speech and sight, the soul with the prophet David then implores God saying: 'Turn away my eyes lest they behold vanity.'[2] Let souls look upon the highest truth, the Creator of all that is, and let them not look at the vanity to which sensual passion invites. The tongue will be a difficult gate to guard, and here the prophet beseeches the Lord to put a barrier with his hand, for where truth is concerned, the two gates provided by nature, that is the lips and the teeth, are not sufficient to shut in such a fierce lioness if God does not bind her with his power. Finally, having meditated on these and other dangers, the soul moves on to consider the wonderful reward which the Lord promises—that if you are pure you shall see for ever the king of majesty in his glory.

When one has heard this, without the slightest hesitation and with the keenness of awakened love and contempt for all this deceitful world, esteeming all the things of its wealth and honour as dung, and longing for the joys which are eternal, one says with the prophet: 'O my God, when shall I come before thy divine presence?'[3]

Here you can see, dear brother, from how small a piece of reading the meditation, which seemed to be a brief, trifling thing, has increased and grown. This meditation the prophet David said he

---

[1] *Invencibles.*   [2] Psalm 118:37 [D].   [3] Cf. Psalm 41:2.

3

practised, pondering over all God's works, because, as in all of them the wisdom, power and goodness of the Creator shine forth, so in them all the omnipotent Lord who created them may be meditated upon.

OROSIUS: This way of meditating would seem suitable for learned men who know how to draw profit from this style and from many others, but how is he who never had much learning, to learn to meditate?

AUGUSTINE: Our God is both all powerful and kind, and he will not forsake anyone or refuse them his treasures, if they ask such favours from his divine Majesty—whether it be a very simple soul who asks or a very learned man. What I mean is that more often those who have received less teaching from men of genius attain to more of these secrets we are discussing than wise and very famous learned men. The reason for this is because the time the learned man is wont to waste in intellectual operations, searching for cogent reasons and very subtle questions, he who is less learned uses in loving his Creator and Lord, and in giving him thanks and praise day and night, and he is very sure of that promise of the Gospel where our Redeemer promises to manifest himself to him who loves him.[1] He does not say this to anyone who with presumptuous daring might seek to understand him, but to him who loves him—following the path that is so short and sure, so sweet and pleasant, of holy love. This is the unction which Holy Scripture says is that which teaches the soul all things. So that the humble man—although he is not learned—when he arrives at this second door of the garden which is meditation, should linger a little over some sentence he may have read or heard preached, and, as he turns it over in his heart, the Holy Spirit will teach him what neither art nor human learning can set forth or teach. Now there remains only one more gate through which to enter this glorious garden— and that is mental prayer. Let us pass through it at least quickly.

OROSIUS: What a high gate and how richly built! The flowering wood that is found when one has passed through to the other side would seem to be of a richness beyond all calculation. I shall never weary of hearing prayer talked of, although something was said of it in the last garden. Speak at least briefly of its great power and worth.

AUGUSTINE: Brother, for more than twenty chapters now, in this garden of prayer, you have been considering the instructions

[1] John 14:21.

which our Redeemer, Jesus Christ, gave us on praying. Let it be sufficient that it is a petition that we offer to our God, in which things good for the redemption of our soul are to be asked for. For if reading showed us the heavenly treasure and meditation the work of seeking means to obtain it, prayer with humility asks that we may be favoured by God, recognizing that the powers of the soul are not sufficient to reach so high a purpose. But reflect that if this gate of prayer is so high that it reaches to heaven, as you saw, men have to pass through it in such a way that they lower the head; and they should humiliate themselves, not in any way presuming like the presumptuous learned men of the world, of whom St. Paul says that through lack of humility they perished miserably. Prayer shows the soul great secrets of God, is the guide of our desires and of so many of our works, and finally is the gate which takes us to the desired garden of contemplation. There St. Bernard says that our heart and desire find marvellously pleasant flowers, wonderful coolness and a fountain of the freshest water—and finally our heart finds the tree of life, our Lord Jesus Christ who is very God.

O great God, at the beginning of our journeyings, when we were at the foot of the holy mountain, who should have thought that we had so great a height to climb. Blessed be God, glory be to his infinite majesty who has shown us such great mercies—already we are among the trees of this paradise so greatly desired, already we see the innocent lamb, Jesus, on the cross between two thieves— so gentle, so kind, so forgetful of his sufferings and labours that he asks only for pardon and mercy for those who are crucifying him. We also see the blessed Virgin, his most pure Mother, whom her blessed Son comforts with words of inestimable love. We learn to know his beloved disciple, St. John, whom this King of mercy does not forget, giving him his own Mother to look after—for love, if it admits forgetfulness, no longer deserves or is called by the name of love.

OROSIUS: To see things which are as blessed to contemplate as those we see on this mount of God and in this holy garden, seems to me a thing altogether sublime and almost beyond my compass. Neither do I know where to begin or where to end, what to choose and what to leave aside, when there are jewels so precious and pearls of such great price.

AUGUSTINE: Do not wonder, brother, at experiencing things so new to you, for the reward of contemplatives is the fruit and blessing which of old the prophet David told us was none other than to contemplate Jesus Christ, true God and true man, in this mount and garden, crucified and dying for us on the holy Cross. This is the mercy which we receive from our God after the labours of our journey, that we should contemplate his splendour and majesty, and that in contemplating them, we should experience how tender and sweet he is to his lovers.

BD. JOHN OF ÁVILA
(1500–1569)

John of Ávila was born of a noble and wealthy family at Almodóvar del Campo, in the archdiocese of Toledo. When he was scarcely fourteen, his father sent him to Salamanca to study jurisprudence, but shortly afterwards he felt a call from God to lead a consecrated life. Abandoning his studies, he returned home and began to lead a life of great austerity. After three years spent in this way, a Franciscan who was visiting the house, and so met the boy, marvelled to find so much virtue in one so young and persuaded his parents to send him to Alcalá to pursue a course of study, so that, equipped with the science of theology, he might the better be able to serve God and souls.

At Alcalá John began his studies under Fray Domingo de Soto. His talent and virtues endeared him both to his professor and his fellow students. When his studies were completed, he was ordained priest, thereafter dedicating himself to preaching for which he had special gifts. He was the preacher at the funeral service which led to St. Francis Borgia's conversion. Before beginning his work as a preacher, he distributed all his inheritance among the poor. He refused both ecclesiastical preferment and opportunities of becoming a court chaplain. He began his course of preaching in Seville, moving on to Córdoba where he was particularly successful as he was also in Granada, his next 'station'. In Granada he was greatly helped by the holy example and counsel of Don Gaspar de Ávalos, who was bishop of that see at the time. Leaving Granada, John moved on to other places in Andalusia, going first to Baeza, where he founded the university, and then to Montilla. Returning to Córdoba, he shortly afterwards went to Zafra (1546), where lived the Marquises of Priego, who were his spiritual disciples. At their invitation he went with them to their estates at Priego, passing the rest of his life there.

From the age of fifty until he was sixty-three he was afflicted with great infirmities because of his constant overwork in preaching. Most of the time he had to remain in bed, but he continued to 'preach' in another manner, writing innumerable spiritual letters to nuns and others. He was known as the 'Apostle of Andalusia'. Like St. Teresa, he was denounced to the Inquisition by an enemy, but the inquiry, which was concerned with his spoken words and not his writings, resulted in his complete justification.

The extracts here given are taken from his 'Letters'—the *Cartas Espirituales*. John of Ávila also left us the important *Libro Espiritual*, perhaps better known as *Audi, filia et vide*, some 'Addresses to Priests', a treatise on the Ten Commandments, and one or two other works.

ON PATIENCE—TO A PRIEST FRIEND
(Letter 7 of the *Cartas Espirituales*)

My dear Father:

When I consider your reverence's poor health, with other circumstances which all together go to make up a painful cross for you, I do not wonder that you should complain of me for not helping you to bear it by sometimes writing to you. On the other hand, as I find it wellnigh impossible to do this, by reason of my daily increasing infirmities, it gives me great pain to hear your laments, for they can serve for nothing but to distress me. I entreat your reverence to realize that this is the case, and let us both try to go with our crosses to the Lord who bore his, asking him to give us his grace to bear contentedly whatever he sends us from his hand.

And certainly, my dear Father, I fear that our great love of bodily comfort and the little we have of the true love of Jesus Christ and him crucified makes us think our troubles great and causes us to complain of lack of consolation; for if in truth we hated ourselves for the love of him, as our Lord commands, we should be glad for him to take satisfaction from us by punishing the offences we have committed against him. We should also take it as a singular favour to eat at the same table with him, even if it be gall and vinegar; for his company is such a great good and so much to be desired, that although it be amid torments, it ought to be most highly prized, for by this path is won his company in the kingdom of heaven, where the Lord will grant to those to whom he gave his companionship here and to those who with him drank gall and vinegar, a share in the honey-bread which is his food.

Let your reverence do violence to yourself in the grace of our Lord and put a good face on this suffering, and in what remains of life not expect anything but one trouble after another. The greater the troubles may be, so much the more should you take them as a pledge of your salvation and as signs that rest is near—for it is common knowledge that at the end of the road to go up to the city, there is a hill. And although in one way this is very tiring, for it comes when we are already weary, on the other hand it gives great consolation, because it is the trial which puts an end to trials, when man enters the city of his desires. This final trial which is wont to come with old age is the good wine of the cross, which the Lord keeps to give his friends at the dessert, as when he changed the water into wine. Let your reverence drink it with joy, for it is of this that *inebriamini carissimi*[1] is to be understood; and by means of it let your reverence hope to be one of those of whom it is written: 'They shall be inebriated from the richness of thy house and with the torrent of thy desire thou wilt give them to drink'. Do not think that this day will be long in coming, for our clay is so fragile and it receives so many blows that it will be broken when we least think, and we shall say: 'The snare is broken and we are freed.'[2]

TO A PRIEST
(Letter 14 of the *Cartas Espirituales*)

May Christ constrain your reverence that you fail not in his service, for all our good consists in being loyal to him. It is a labour to look to oneself alone and a labour more than doubled when one looks to oneself and others. Few there are who can fulfil these two obligations according as each one exerts a greater or lesser attraction so that they fail in neither. A man who is inclined to look to himself finds it very hard to understand his duty to his neighbour; that he should leave all else in view of that neighbour's present necessities, for here lies his greater and primary obligation. There are other persons who, seeing the good they do to others, forget themselves; and these run a greater risk. What I desire of your reverence is that, as on the night of his Passion our sovereign Master rose to pray, and then returned to his disciples and from them went back again to his prayer, mingling the one life with the other, so you should do, not neglecting either for the sake of the other. Clearly do I see how heavy is this charge which you sustain with difficulty, and how steeled and armed one must be to derive profit from it and not to take harm. But the difficulty of the task should not throw us into despair, but make us more careful and watchful, as with something of special importance.

Great is the weakness which men show in our days, when of those who say they serve God, there is scarcely a man who will put his shoulder to things that are difficult. We want everything to our liking and that what we say may be accepted forthwith. For we are exceedingly weak in many things, though we cry out in reproach at the weaknesses of others; we are soft to our own frailties though angry at those of others, instead of being patient with those of others and having a fervent zeal against ourselves.

---

[1] 'Be inebriated, my dearly beloved' (Canticle of Canticles 5:1 [D]).
[2] Psalm 123:7.

This being so, it is often necessary in the affairs of God to undergo the sweat of death, and his servant has to be, as it were, insensitive to pain, suffering and calling upon the Lord. He who hopes in God and fights against the devil must be persevering and magnanimous; for those who are not so either turn aside from the way or go along in such weakness and with so many falls, that it is as if they had not moved. Let your reverence walk forward with your cross and invoke the Crucified who died for souls, in the firm belief that he does not forget them, however much he lets them suffer—but he wants the cross to cost us something, that he may do us the favour of taking us as helpers in such high work, and to reward us as the Father did him. The work is his, we are his ministers, and he wants to prove our faith, charity and patience, so that we do not see the profit we desire to reap immediately, and thus he shows us mercy and that in no small measure, even when it seems as if he does not hear us.

What your reverence ought to say to such disconsolate folk is, that they should take the ten commandments of God and the five[1] of the Church, and keep them—and with these they will be saved. If they want to do more, all well and good, provided they do not think that if it should happen that they fail in doing more, they are therefore lost. Almost all the harm comes to them from their being desirous of devotion and pious feelings, and in this they think their salvation consists; if they were to lay as much stress upon keeping God's commandments as on these other things, it would go better with them; for they would succeed in this and would have peace. Let your reverence set down these things for them in writing and tell them that they should think of that and it will go well with them. And if they want to pray, let them do so, on condition that they reflect that they are thus going to obey God, who commands us to pray even if we obtain no consolation. Let them read and recite their vocal prayers, thinking of what they are saying, and let them look to the keeping of the commandments, and let them learn to be thankful to God who gives them grace to fulfil them; and if they sometimes slip, let them have recourse to the remedy of the contrite and humble heart, and believe that the blood of Jesus Christ cleanses our sins, and, going to confession, they will be at peace. Let them not want to do violence to themselves to carry all this out, for sanctity is the gift of God. Let them do as many good people do, who content themselves with keeping the

[1] The commandments of the Church now number six, but in Bd. John's time five. Cf. *Catholic Encyclopedia*, Vol. IV.

law of the Lord with a staunch will, without sighing after feelings
of devotion. When the Lord wants something more, he will make
his will known. May your reverence pray to God for me, as I do
for you.

TO A GIRL WHO WANTED TO ENTER A CONVENT
(Letter 9 of the *Cartas Espirituales*)

The favour that Jesus Christ our Lord has shown you in giving
you the desire to leave the vanities and false pleasures of the world
is so great that if he in his mercy does not give you light to recognize
it as such and strength to keep to it, you will not be able to do so.
It is he who has given you this resolve, for the sons of Adam only
want to enjoy this world and care little about the next. Blessed for
ever may he be who has saved you from deception about that which
deceives many, and has given you to understand that it is better
to leave this world than to enjoy it, and to be espoused to Jesus
Christ rather than to any earthly husband. Learn to appreciate this
favour, consider yourself as fortunate in being called to espousals
such as these and pray earnestly that he who confers this favour
upon you may give you grace to know how to keep it and may
strengthen you to take firmly on your shoulders the sweet yoke
of our Lord which will be placed upon you in the convent. Even if
trials should come along, hold them of little account in exchange
for being the spouse of Christ, and hold it as certain that although
you may find some trials there, those which you leave outside are
greater, since for one of its pleasures the world gives a hundred
trials, and for one trial borne for Christ, he gives a hundred
rewards.

Try hard to be humble with all, holding yourself to be less than
they, for the Son of God prostrated himself at the feet of the
Apostles, and washed them for our example. If you know how to
humble yourself in this world, you will be exalted in the next,
and the more you lower yourself here, the greater will be your
glory in heaven. Remember that the Lord says:[1] 'Learn of me for
I am meek and humble of heart.' Fix these words in your inmost
heart and they will be of much profit to you all your life, for the
humble person is at the service of all and the meek suffer all things.
He who humbles himself the Lord recognizes as his son, just as
the devil recognizes the proud and angry as his own. Be a lover of
obedience, for, obeying those set over you, you obey Christ, and

[1] Matthew 11 : 29.

if you make good progress in this virtue, you have found paradise upon earth. And because at the beginning this is sufficient, I do not say more to you until, after you have actually entered the convent, you tell me how you are getting on. May it please the mercy of that Lord who has called you for himself to perféct in you what he has begun, so that you may serve him perfectly in this life and afterwards enjoy him to the full in heaven.

TO A YOUNG LADY: THAT IT IS NOT FOR MAN TO
CHOOSE HIS CROSS, BUT TO CARRY THE ONE GOD
GIVES HIM
(Letter 32 of the *Cartas Espirituales*)

If the troubles that come to us were those we sought, they would not be troubles, and we should be deprived of the company of our Redeemer's cross, which is the greatest ill that could happen to us. That which is most irksome to us has to come to us, for thus our self-will has to be cured until nothing that comes to us is irksome, and then we shall be the servants of Jesus Christ, who said:[1] 'Not my will but thine be done'. Since, then, he in his great mercy takes the trouble to send you what is for the health of your soul, do not receive it as an injury which wounds, but as a medicine which heals. Give thanks to your Saviour and brace yourself with fortitude to suffer greater things, for there has not come to us yet what usually comes to those who are true servants of the Crucified, nor what we ought to desire. All that comes to us from without, we must think that God sends from on high with his mercy and reflect within ourselves that we deserve very much more; we must not flee from our purgatory, however much it hurts. When God wills you to begin truly to suffer and sends you what you would most avoid suffering, then you may be confident that you are loved by him and may hope to see the face of the Lord with joy. The way to God does not consist in words, and therefore one should not faint under trials, but do violence to oneself in God, who sends us war to crown us with victory. Recollect yourself in him in prayer for a long space until, if needs be, you sweat drops of blood, setting before your eyes the example of Jesus Christ our Lord, who prayed three times and with so much travail, but was not heard immediately until the blood ran down and watered the earth.

Submit yourself entirely to the will of God, and turn yourself

[1] Luke 22:42.

round like a piece of clay and say to the Lord: I am clay and you, Lord, the potter: make of me what you will. Let not God find you clothed with your own will, but utterly denuded of it; for however small the thing your will clings to, if it is not mortified it will give you no small trouble and discomfort. You are Christ's by a most just purchase. Do not let it be a trouble to you that you are so, and do not seek to escape from his treatment, but with all your heart ask him to take your will for himself where he knows and wants it and not where it wants to go, even if it should be to suffer extreme disgrace before the eyes of the whole world. See that you put this lesson the Lord has sent you to good account, for otherwise he may not send you what is fitting for you but what you want, and it will be to your harm. Gather up hope in God and fight manfully, for the friendship of our Lord is worthy of this and of more, and he who does not suffer much for the beloved cannot boast of being a lover. May God strengthen you so much that you may be adequate to strengthen the weak and console the sad, and may show perfect obedience to his holy will and perfect faith in his goodness. Amen.

LUIS DE GRANADA
(1504–1588)

Luis of Granada was born in that city in 1504. He was a contemporary of St. Teresa (1515–1582), whom he outlived by six years. His parents were from Galicia. They were poor and when he was only five, his father died. His mother supported herself and her son by taking in washing for the Dominican priory of Santa Cruz in Granada, and Luis entered the Order there in 1525.[1] He was sent to study in Valladolid, where he became acquainted with Melchior Cano. He played a principal part in the restoration of the Dominican priory at Córdoba and it was there that he met and came under the influence of Bd. John of Ávila (see p. 57). He later went to found a house of the Order at Badajoz and from there to Portugal, where he was offered, and refused, a bishopric. In 1577 he was made Provincial of his Order in Portugal (then, as now, a separate kingdom from Spain—the annexation took place in 1580). Luis de Granada was a preacher of considerable reputation, much admired by Philip II. In his last years his eyesight failed, he became almost blind and had to depend on others for the services of reading and dictation.

It was not until comparatively late in life that Fray Luis began to write. His output was considerable and his numerous writings include works in Latin and Portuguese as well as in Castilian. His work is rated highly by literary critics and did much to enrich the prose of the Golden Age. Among his important writings is the 'Guide for Sinners', from which we give one extract. It is a treatise on the moral virtues and their contrary vices, written at Badajoz. The 'Memorial of the Christian Life', from which the second extract is taken, is a treatise on asceticism which at the same time touches on certain aspects of mysticism. Luis de Granada also wrote lives of Bd. John of Ávila and Brother Bartholomew of the Martyrs. His monumental 'Introduction to the Symbol of the Faith', an exposition of the Creed, was begun when he was nearly eighty. Some of Luis de Granada's works were translated into English and were popular among Anglicans in the late sixteenth and seventeenth centuries.

REMEDIES AGAINST AVARICE
(from 'Guide for Sinners', Book 2, Ch. 5)

Avarice is an inordinate desire of wealth. For this reason and with some justification, not only is the man who steals held to be avaricious, but also he who inordinately covets things which belong

---

[1] Some authorities give the year as 1524.

to others or who clings tenaciously to what is his own. This is the vice the Apostle condemns when he says:[1] 'Those who desire to be rich fall into temptations and snares of the devil and into many futile and harmful desires which bring men to perdition. For covetousness is the root of all evils.' The malice of this vice could not be more greatly emphasized than by this saying; for we are thereby given to understand that he who is subject to this vice is the slave of all the others.

When, then, this vice tempts your heart, you can arm yourself against it with the following considerations. Firstly consider, you who are avaricious, that when your Lord and God came down from heaven to this world, he did not will to possess these riches which you desire; on the contrary, he so loved poverty that he willed to take flesh of a poor and humble Virgin and not of some exalted and mighty queen. And when he was born he did not want to be lodged in great palaces nor to be put into a soft bed or delicately fashioned cradle, but into a manger, wretched and hard, where he lay upon straw. Afterwards, so long as he lived in this life, he always loved poverty and despised riches; for he chose for his Apostles and ambassadors, not princes or great lords, but some poor fishermen. What greater mockery, then, can there be than for the worm to want to be rich, when the Lord of everything created willed to be poor for its sake?

Consider also the vileness of your heart when, although your soul was created to the image of God and redeemed by his blood (in comparison with which the whole world is nothing), you are willing to lose it for a little gain. God did not give his life for the whole world in general, but gave it for the soul of man; a soul, then, is of greater value than the whole world. True riches are not gold, or silver, or precious stones. That which all the philosophers of the world despised, do you, disciple of Christ who are called to a greater good, hold to be a thing so important that you make yourself a slave of it? Because, as St. Jerome says,[2] he is the slave of riches who guards them like a slave; but he who shakes off this yoke from himself, distributes them like a lord.

Think also that, as the Saviour says, no one can serve two masters: that is, God and riches; and that the mind of man cannot freely contemplate God if he walks through the riches of the world with his mouth wide open. Spiritual delights shun the heart that is busied with temporal ones, and it is impossible to unite together

[1] I Timothy 6:9.   [2] *Com. in Habac.*, c. 3.

vain things with true, lofty with base, eternal with temporal, and spiritual with carnal, so that you may enjoy both together. Consider, moreover, that the more prosperously earthly things turn out for you, the more wretched you will be in the time to come; because here you even boast of entrusting yourself to that false happiness which is offered to you. If you only knew how much misfortune that fragile prosperity brings with it! The love of riches torments us more by our very desire of them than it delights us in the use of them; for it entangles the soul in different temptations, ensnares it in many cares, entices it with vain delights, provokes it to sin and prevents its quiet and repose. Over and above all this, riches are never acquired without toil, nor are they possessed without care, nor are they lost without pain; and, worst of all, they are seldom acquired without offending God; because (as the proverb says) the rich man is either evil or is the inheritor of evil.

Consider, too, what great folly it is continually to desire those things which it is certain, even if they are all put together, cannot satisfy your appetite; but rather stir it up and increase it, as the thirst of him who has the dropsy is increased by drinking; because, however much you have, you always covet what you lack and are always sighing for more. The sad heart thus roams through the things of the world, grows weary and is not satisfied; it drinks and its thirst is not quenched, because it makes no account of what it has, but only of what more it might have; and its vexation over what is beyond its reach is no less than its contentment over what it possesses. Its heart is no more satisfied with gold than with air. Of this St. Augustine very rightly says: 'What is this covetousness of men that is so insatiable, when even the brute beasts observe a measure in their desires? For they hunt when they suffer hunger; but when they are satisfied, then they desist from hunting.' The avarice of the rich, alone, puts no measure to its desires, for it always plunders and is never satisfied.

Reflect, moreover, that where there is much wealth, there are many persons to consume it, many to waste it, many to squander and steal it. What does the richest man in the world derive from his riches more than what is necessary for his life? But for this you need not be anxious if you put your hope in God and recommend yourself to his providence: for he never forsakes those who hope in him, and he who made man with the necessity of eating does not will him to perish of hunger. How could it be that God who feeds the little birds and clothes the lilies should forsake man—especially when what is sufficient to remedy the necessity is so little? Life is short and death comes on apace. What need have you of so much provision for such a short journey? For what do you want so much wealth, when the less you have, the more freely and unencumbered you will travel? When you reach the end of the journey, it will not go any the less well with you if you arrive poor, than with the rich who arrive heavily loaded; rather when the journey is ended, there will remain less for you to feel you are leaving and less for which to give account to God—whereas those who are more wealthy at the end of the journey will not leave the heaps of gold which they loved so much without great anguish and not without great peril will they give account of the much they possessed.

Consider, moreover, O man of avarice, for whom you are heaping up such great wealth, for it is certain that as you came into this world with nothing, so also you have to go forth from it. You were born into this life poor, you will leave it poor. This you should think of frequently, for, as St. Jerome says, he who remembers that he has to die, easily despises all things. At the point of death you will leave all worldly goods and carry away with you only the works you have done, good or evil—wherefore you will lose all heavenly riches, if you held them of little account so long as you lived, and gave all your efforts to acquiring and keeping worldly wealth. For your things will then be divided into three parts; the body will be handed over to the worms, the soul to the demons and your material goods to your heirs, who may perchance be ungrateful, or wasteful or evil. It will therefore be better, in accordance with our Saviour's counsel, to distribute such goods to the poor who will carry them before you (as great lords do when they travel, sending their riches before them). What greater folly than to leave your wealth where you will never return and not to send it on before you where you will live for ever?

Consider, again, that the sovereign Governor of the world (like the prudent father of a family) has distributed both offices and riches in such a manner that some are ordained to rule and others to be ruled; some that they should distribute what is necessary and others that they should receive it. Since you are one of those who are so placed as to make distribution from your surplus wealth, do you think it is lawful for you to keep for yourself what you have received for many? For, as St. Basil says, the bread which you store away belongs to the poor, and the garment you hide, to the naked, and the money you bury, to the needy. Know then for certain that you have robbed of their goods all those whom you could have benefited with your surplus wealth but did not so benefit. Realize, then, that the goods you have received from God are remedies for human misery and not instruments of an evil life. See, then, that when all things turn out prosperously for you, you do not forget who it is who gives them to you; and that you do not make the remedies for other people's misery the subject of vainglory. It is not exile you should seek to love, brother, but the fatherland; and of the equipment and provisions for the journey, do not make obstacles as you travel along the road; nor through much loving of the light of the moon, despise the light of midday; nor turn what are helps for the present life into everlasting death. Live content with the lot that falls to you, remembering that the Apostle says: Having sufficient for our maintenance and clothing wherewith to cover us, with this we are content. Because (as St. Chrysostom says) the servant of God has not to clothe himself, either to appear well or for the delight of his flesh, but to comply with justice, and all other things will be granted to you, because God who loves to give you the great things will not deny you the small ones. Remember that it is not poverty which is a virtue, but the love of poverty.

The poor who are voluntarily poor are like Christ who, being rich, made himself poor for us. But those who live in poverty of necessity and bear it with patience, and despise the riches which they have not, of this forced poverty make a virtue. As the poor by their poverty are conformed to Christ, so the rich by their alms are converted to Christ, for it was not only the poor shepherds who found Christ but also the wise and mighty when they offered him their treasures. You, then, who have sufficient wealth, give alms to the poor, because when you give to them, it is Christ who receives it. And hold it for certain that in heaven (where your everlasting dwelling is to be) what you now give them is stored up for you: but if on this earth you hide your treasures, do not expect to find anything where you put nothing. How then can you call that which a man cannot take with him, but rather loses against his will his riches? Spiritual riches, on the contrary, are real wealth, for they do not forsake their owner even at his death; neither can anyone deprive him of them against his will.

WHAT MAN OUGHT TO DO FOR HIS NEIGHBOUR
(from 'Guide for Sinners', Book 2, ch. 16)

The second part of justice concerns what a man ought to do for his neighbour, namely, to use toward him that mercy and charity which God commands us. How important this part of the subject is and how much it is recommended to us in the Sacred Scriptures (which are the masters and guides of our life) will scarcely be believed unless one reads them. Read the Prophets, read the Gospels, read the sacred Epistles, and you will see this matter so highly spoken of that you will be astonished. In Isaias, God places a very considerable part of justice in the good treatment of our neighbours within the setting of charity. Thus when the Jews complained, saying: 'Why, Lord, do we fast and you have not regarded our fasts; why do we afflict our souls and you have taken no account of it?', God answers them: 'Because in the day of your fast you live according to your own will and not to mine: and you oppress and harass all your debtors. You fast, but not from lawsuits and disputes, nor from doing ill to your neighbour. That, then, is not the fast that pleases me, but this: break your contracts and bonds of usury; remove from the poor the burdens with which you have bound them down; allow the afflicted and the necessitous to go free and pull them out from under the yoke that you have placed upon them; of any loaf you have, share half with the poor man, and take the needy and strangers into your house. When you do this and open your heart to the needy man and help him and give him sufficiently, then I will give you such and such good things':[1]— which he continues very lavishly right to the end of this chapter. You see from this, then, brother, what that is in which God makes a great part of true justice to consist and how mercifully he wills that we should behave towards our neighbours in this respect.

What shall I say, then, of the Apostle St. Paul? In which of his Epistles is not this the greatest of his recommendations? What praises he gives to charity, how greatly he exalts it, how frequently he recounts all its excellences, how he places it before all other virtues, saying that this is the most excellent way there is for going to God. And not content with this he says in one place that charity is the bond of perfection; in another he says that it is the end of all the commandments; in another that he who loves his neighbour has fulfilled the law. What greater praises, then, of a virtue could be looked for than these? Who is the man desirous of knowing with what kind of works he can please God, who is not full of admiration and love for this virtue, and determined to ordain and direct all his works to it?

Even over and above all this, there remains the Canonical

[1] Cf. Isaias 58.

Epistle of that great beloved and lover of Christ, St. John the Evangelist, in which there is nothing more often repeated, nor more recommended, nor more praised than this virtue; and what he did in this epistle, history says he was doing all his life. When asked why he repeated this phrase so many times, he answered, 'Because if it is properly fulfilled, it is sufficient for our salvation.'

OF THE LOVE AND CONFIDENCE WITH WHICH
THE HOLY EUCHARIST SHOULD BE APPROACHED
(from 'Memorial of the Christian Life', Treatise 2)

Our love and confidence will be enkindled by considering further that this Lord, great as he is in majesty and in justice and in the abhorrence of sin, is equally great in his goodness, mercy and loving-kindness towards sinners. For it was this that made him come down from heaven to earth, clothe himself in our flesh, going along roads and highways in search of sinners, eating in company with them. It was this that made him say that to save them was his food and his delight. For them he fasted, journeyed, sweated, toiled, kept watch, rose at break of day and suffered innumerable persecutions and contradictions from the world; for them he journeyed and preached by day, and for them he kept watch and prayed by night; for them the gateway of his compassion was always open, in such a way that he neither rejected nor sent away anyone however wretched and outcast he might be. Finally, he so much desired the salvation and healing of such sinners, that to see them healed, he did not hesitate to put himself on a cross between two thieves and shed all the blood he had for them. And not content with this (so that when the course of his mortal life was finished, there should not be wanting another such refuge for them as he had been on earth), he left and ordained this divine sacrament in which he himself remains with us; in order that all this race of men so greatly in need might always have the same help and the same resource available for their wants. Thus the very reason that caused him to die also made him institute this sacrament, because, just as love was what brought him from heaven to earth, and made him place himself in the hands of sinners, so it is love which now makes him come once more into the world in this way and which places him in the same hands.

From this it is clear that on his side the cause of this mighty work was none other than his immense love; and from our side, nothing else but our great need. It came out of his mercy alone.

Whence it follows that this divine sacrament is the common remedy of the just and sinners, for not only is it the food of the healthy but also the medicine of the sick. Not only is it the life of the living but also the resurrection of the dead, for (as St. Augustine says) this bread not only nourishes those it finds living but also at times raises the dead.

On what ground, then, can anyone forbid me from partaking of this mystery?

This is a royal hospital instituted by the divine mercy and endowed with the blood of Christ as the universal remedy for all those who are sick and in need. Why, then, because I am ill should I be excluded from it? Rather for the very reason that I am ill (if I desire to be healed) I have the greater obligation to have recourse to it. For if I am ill, here I shall be cured; if I am weak, here I shall be strengthened; if I am blind, here I shall be given light; if I am poor, here it will be given to me to eat my fill, and if I am naked, here shall I be clothed and my nakedness covered.

This is what those who with similar excuses hold aloof from this sacrament and keep others away from the use of it will never understand or do not want to understand; for they do not face the fact that this divine mystery was instituted not only as the food of those who are whole, but also as a medicine for those who are sick; not only for the delight and strengthening of the just, but also for the medicine and strengthening of penitents. Whoever feels himself most weak has the greater need of it, and on this count the weak are able to live without it far less than the strong; because the strong can persevere for longer time without this help, but he whose soul is sick to death and who is so weak and so lacking in strength that when he turns his eyes a little away from God, he immediately begins to fail, what shall restrain such a man from falling headlong if he does not take advantage of this help? And especially for this reason did the Saviour have compassion on this sort of man when, speaking of this mystery in figure, he said: 'If I let them go on their way fasting, they will faint by the way, for some of them have come from afar.' Because there is no doubt that as then, those who had come from afar stood in greater danger than those who came from nearby (because their day's journey was longer), so also now those who are weakest and those who have the greatest way to go before reaching the perfection of the love of God suffer most. And since this heavenly bread was ordained as a remedy for such, it is not presumption, but very salutary counsel, that he who is desirous of a remedy for his ills should have recourse to the physician and take advantage of the medicine which he ordained for this with no lesser love than at the cost of blood.

One of the great faults of men, indeed, and one of which they will have to give much account on the day of reckoning, is in regard to the blood of Christ—by which I mean the not having cared to take advantage of the remedies which were instituted for us by means of that precious blood, of which this sacrament is the greatest. If a king had built a wonderful hospital, providing in great abundance all things necessary for the cure of the sick; and if after the work was finished with much expense and trouble on his part, there were no sick people who cared to be cured there, would he not consider this as perverse when he found all his intentions and labours frustrated? Well, then, the King of heaven is no less offended if after having given with his own blood such a great and costly remedy as this, we do not want to take advantage of it, since by so doing (for as much as lies in our part) we frustrate all his purposes and labours. And this is the manner of offence which the Lord pointed out in the parable of the Supper when, everything necessary for the banquet being prepared, he sent to call the guests and they would not come. Against them he pronounced that terrible sentence of excommunication, saying: 'Amen I say to you that none of those men who were called shall taste of my supper.'

This being so, then, what reason can you have for excusing yourself from this banquet? If you say that you are a sinner, he is no longer a sinner who desires to be just and is sore troubled at having been a sinner; because, as St. Jerome says,[1] past sins do not damn you if they do not please you. If you say that you are fallen and cast down, he can no longer be called fallen who is troubled because he fell, and stretches out his hand that he may be raised up. If you say that you are unworthy to draw near to so great a mystery, you are no small fool if you think that there is anyone in the world completely worthy of approaching it; because it was for this that the Lord willed to give himself to little ones, for thereby the glory of his goodness would be made more clearly manifest and therefore he longed to communicate himself to such as these. Thus, having given due consideration to all this, you will see clearly that not only do you not offend the Lord by drawing near to him, but you would rather offend him much more in not wanting to take advantage of the remedy which he instituted for such as yourself. And with these and other like considerations, the desire with which we ought to approach this mystery is enkindled.

[1] *Sup. Marcum*, c. 6, tom. 9.

PART OF A SERMON FOR THE FEAST OF THE ASSUMPTION

Among all the feasts of Our Lady which the holy Catholic Church celebrates, this is the most glorious; because in all the others, however great they may be, there is always mingled some trace of trouble and sorrow, because in this life all there is takes on the complexion of the place where we are, which is a place of exile and a vale of tears; but this feast, which is no longer of those belonging to this life, is free from such attributes; and not only do we not find in it what we do in the others, a tinge of sorrow, but rather a release from all affliction.

If we look at the letter only, the Gospel[1] which is sung on this day is not suited to this feast; but if we consider the spirit hidden beneath the letter, none more suitable could be sung on this occasion. It tells how Jesus Christ entered a hamlet called Bethany situated close by Mount Olivet, and was the guest of an honest woman named Martha who had a sister called Mary. When the Lord went in to the house, he was well received by the sisters, and as he sat down to rest from the fatigue of his journey, Mary sat at his feet, oblivious to all that had to be made ready for Christ and those who were with him, quite carried away by seeing the Lord and hanging on the words that came from his lips. The elder sister was busy providing bodily sustenance for the Lord and his companions, and the younger feeding her own soul with heavenly teaching. And as she received spiritual nourishment into her soul, so also she ministered with her loving devotion to the soul of Jesus Christ, our sweet Lord: so that Martha [was] completely occupied in getting bodily nourishment for Christ and those who were with him, while Mary was wholly enraptured, receiving from Christ nourishment for her own soul, and with this loving rapture, also ministering to the soul of Christ most delectable food.

If we look at the letter from within the spirit the Blessed Virgin performed both these services for God far better than these two sisters, for she was more excellent than they. The excellence of these great services of hers to the Lord tells us what the reward given to her for them today was to be. These sisters were important ladies; they had a mansion there. The most holy Virgin is (in a

---

[1] The reference is to the former Gospel for the feast.

spiritual sense) the fortress and secure castle where the Lord of all was received when he entered this world in a new manner. She served him as Martha and contemplated him as Mary: she chose the better part, which she will enjoy for ever. We shall explain how she was Martha and Mary, and how she ministered to the Lord with absolute perfection in both ways. . . .

ALONSO DE MADRID

Alonso de Madrid was an early sixteenth-century Spanish Franciscan, the dates of whose birth and death are not known with certainty. He was probably from the province of Castile, or perhaps from that of Cartagena. From the maturity of his writings, we may conclude that he cannot have been born later than the last quarter of the fifteenth century. The work for which he is best known—the *Arte para Servir a Dios* ('The Art of Serving God') was first printed at Seville in 1521. It had an enormous success and was translated into Latin by a Belgian Dominican father. In 1555, a French edition was published at Toulouse. The *Arte* is mentioned by St. Teresa in her 'Autobiography' as very suitable for those who are at the first stage of mental prayer. The language is clear and the metaphors and similes are taken from everyday life.

The work of Alonso of Madrid is rated highly by literary critics. He also wrote: 'Seven Meditations for Holy Week', a 'Treatise on Christian Doctrine' and a 'Memorial of the Life of Jesus Christ'. A work published in Burgos in 1542, the 'Mirror of Illustrious Personages', is likewise ascribed to his pen.

'On Patience' is from the *Arte*. The four prayers of Alonso's were printed at the end of the edition of 1621.

ON PATIENCE
(from 'The Art of Serving God', Pt. 2, ch. 7)

The other virtue[1] which our Redeemer and Master Jesus Christ wants us to learn from him is patience. It is so much a sister of humility that they are almost always together, and usually where one is found, the other is found with it. As we have said when treating of humility, we should always have before our eyes the patience of our Master. For who, when he deserves it and knows he deserves it, will complain that he is injured and hurt by ill-treatment, if he considers with what meekness Christ suffered all that persecution, ignominy, abasement, pain and torture, with the most humiliating death of the Cross, when, besides being Lord of all, he was the most sensitive and delicate in body of all those ever born? Who will not suffer trials and troubles with meekness, when they are offered him as a remedy and satisfaction for his own faults,

[1] The first was humility.

75

if he considers how his God suffered incomparably greater ones for those of others and in so doing provided a remedy for our ills?

How we can acquire patience by another means and still use this consideration is already set out in sufficient detail and exemplified earlier, and so we refer you to that and will only treat here of the great riches that can always be drawn from any occasion of impatience that presents itself to us. Let us take as our example a matter of great annoyance. You suspect with some slight reason that someone has said something evil of you falsely. Three blows are struck at your soul by this suspicion, one of misjudgment, another of most irritating impatience and another of hatred against him whom you suspect of having said it. The servant of God who has begun to learn goodness and the art of serving him should defend himself from these dangerous blows and shake them off in such a manner that not only is he not wounded by any of them, but rather in the case of each one, derives much profit from his victory. At the first blow, asking God for his help in the struggle, he should turn his back, bending his will so that it does not even wish to consent to judge rashly, reflecting how it is forbidden to us to judge by the great Judge himself: and thus we should joyfully leave judgment alone and not usurp it to ourselves. Against the second blow one should protect oneself, with the grace of God and his help gathering up all one's strength and firmness to receive it without its hurting him. Thus he will be able to be at ease and rejoice at the pain which was to injure and afflict him: for his sins merit nothing but pain and affliction. And the more he wills to be at ease and to rejoice at that injury and pain, so much the less will the devil fight him with the weapon of impatience, in order not to give him the occasion of much merit. The better to prevail in this, a man can gather greater strength by calling to mind what has been said of hatred of self in the third chapter. Against the third blow, which is the hatred with which the person has injured us, we shall defend ourselves by forcing the will to produce a very special act of love towards that person for the love of God, for we are able by our great liberty to will and not to will whatever we hold as good, and to give to the act the end we would, as has already been said.

In the same way, as we have shown how to provide for the defence against these three blows, given on that trifling occasion, we ought also to defend ourselves effectively and with due attention in all life offers us of greater trials and tribulations—so that patience may always remain in our soul without hurting us. I say due

attention and due effectiveness, and I want it to be understood
here and everywhere that without the Lord's grace and his merciful
help, no attention or effectiveness can be good. In this all that is
to be of value must have its foundation, and for this we must always
ask our Lord, beginning by this and returning to it as the true
principle and source of all our good.

It is also to be recommended that we should have a great love
and esteem for patience, keeping it always in mind, as Jesus Christ
our Master said, for that is what makes a man lord of his soul. He
who becomes master of patience possesses himself wholly and has
entire power over himself, so that he can command and dispose of
himself as he would. Jesus Christ in saying this points out its
counterpart most clearly. The impatient man is his own slave,
possessed, dominated by and subject to his appetite and open to
the attack of trouble or vengeance.

FOUR PRAYERS
I
A most devout prayer

O Jesus Christ, my Redeemer, I ask of thy divine Majesty that
thou wouldst show favour to me, an unworthy sinner, and wouldst
keep me all the days of my life. God of Abraham, God of Isaac,
God of Jacob, have mercy on me and send Saint Michael the Archangel to my help that he may guard me, favour me, visit me and
defend me from all my enemies, visible and invisible, fleshly,
spiritual and temporal. Holy Michael Archangel, defend me against
the temptations of the devil that I may not be overcome and may
not have cause to accuse myself on the final judgment day before
the Majesty of God.

Holy Michael Archangel, I ask thee, by the grace which thou didst
merit to obtain from the only-begotten Son of God, our Lord, that
thou wouldst keep me away from all those evils present, past and
future which I do not know how to guard myself from. I place as
my intercessor before his divine Majesty our Lady the glorious
Virgin Mary, with all the heavenly hosts. St. Michael, St. Gabriel,
St. Raphael and all the holy angels and archangels of God, help me,
an unworthy sinner. I ask all the powers of heaven that no enemy
may overcome me in the way, nor on the water, nor in the fire, nor
in the house, nor out of it, nor travelling along the road, nor
returning, nor keeping watch, nor sleeping, nor eating, nor in
whatever I may be doing. Behold the Cross of our Lord Jesus
Christ. Flee, hostile powers. The lion of the tribe of Juda, the root

of David, has conquered—Our Saviour Jesus Christ, who didst save the world by thy most precious blood and death on the Cross, I ask thee, my Redeemer, that thou wouldst save me today and all the days of my life, and in the final hour of death. May the Cross of our Lord Jesus Christ help me. May the Cross of our Lord Jesus Christ keep me from all evil. May the Cross of our Lord Jesus Christ save me all the days of my life. In the name of the Father, and of the Son, and of the Holy Spirit. Amen.

II
Prayer to the Cross

May the Cross of my Lord Jesus Christ be with me. The Cross of my Lord Jesus Christ is that which I ever adore, the Cross of my Lord Jesus Christ is my true hope and salvation, the Cross of my Lord Jesus Christ overcomes all evil visions. The Cross of my Lord Jesus Christ conquers the bonds of death. May the Cross of my Lord Jesus Christ be favourable to me. May the Cross of my Lord Jesus Christ set me free from all evils. May the Cross of my Lord Jesus Christ deliver me from all the adversities of the whole world. May the Cross of my Lord Jesus Christ save me and when the evil spirits see me may they depart: by the sign of the holy Cross may all evil temptations depart from me, and through the sign of the Holy Cross may I receive all happiness and joy. Amen.

III
For the Relief of Sickness

My Lord Jesus Christ, who through thy Apostle Bartholomew didst heal the sick in the temple of King Astator and the daughter of King Polymius[1] who was possessed of a devil: so I ask thee, my Redeemer Jesus Christ, that through his intercession I may be freed from this sickness, thou who livest and reignest for ever and ever. Amen.

IV
Act of Contrition

(which it will be very profitable to make many times a day, especially on rising and going to bed, to obtain the pardon of one's sins)

Praised be the most Holy Sacrament and the most pure Conception of our Lady.

[1] Cf. Lectio v, Noct. II for feast of St. Bartholomew.

O Lord God Almighty, Creator and my most sweet Father, because thou art what thou art, and because I love and cherish thee above all things, it grieves me to have offended thee, and I firmly resolve not to offend thee more, and to go to confession; and I ask thy pardon for the offences I have committed and hope to obtain it through the merits of Jesus Christ, thy most holy Son and my Redeemer. Amen.

(It is recommended that these words be said with the greatest sorrow for having offended our Lord, and with the greatest possible sincerity.)

SAINT TERESA OF ÁVILA
(1515–1582)

Her life is well known. It will be recalled that she was a Spanish girl of good family who entered the Carmelite convent of the Incarnation at Ávila more from a sense of duty than because it was her heart's desire. There she led a more or less tepid life for twenty years more, taking advantage of the relaxations from austerity which the customs of the time allowed—relaxations which were in part due to the convent's economic difficulties—until she experienced a conversion that gave her the grace gradually to become a saint. This was not all. She was called upon by God to reform the Carmelite Order, both of nuns and of friars, which had fallen sadly from its first fervour. This meant continual journeys up and down Spain, travelling in uncomfortable carts over rough roads sometimes deep in mud, sleeping in inns where the food was unpalatable and the beds not always clean (no wonder she compared this life to a night in a bad inn), to found the houses of the reform.

St. Teresa was a woman of strong character and of many parts who would have been great in any walk of life. Her mysticism went hand in hand with cool common sense—a quality she valued highly in others. The story of her life may be read in the pages of her 'Autobiography'[1], that of the reform of the Carmelite Order in the 'Book of the Foundations'. St. Teresa's style is homely and discursive and 'The Way of Perfection' and her other writings are eminently readable. Because her writings are so widely known we here give only an extract from one of her lesser-known works.

OF THE SWEET AND DELIGHTFUL LOVE OF GOD
WHICH ARISES FROM HIS DWELLING IN THE SOUL
IN THE PRAYER OF QUIET...
(from 'Meditations on the Canticle of Canticles', ch. 4)

'[For] thy breasts are better than wine, smelling sweet of the best ointments' (Canticle of Canticles 1, 1–2 [D]).

1. What great secrets there are in these words, my daughters! May our Lord allow us to experience what it is so difficult to express. When His Majesty is pleased, of his mercy, to grant this petition of the Bride, the friendship which he begins to enter into

---

[1] English translation by Allison Peers, London, 1946.

with the soul is, as I say, one which only those who experience it
will understand. I have written much about it in two books (which
if it please the Lord you will see after I die) in lengthy detail,
because I think that you will need it, and so here I shall not do more
than touch on the matter. I do not know if I shall manage to find
the same words as those the Lord was pleased to use to explain it.

2. So great a sweetness comes into the interior of the soul that
it feels our Lord very near.

3. This is not only a feeling of devotion, of the sort that moves
to many tears. For although these cause tenderness when we weep
either for the Lord's Passion or on account of our sins, this is not
so important as this prayer of which I speak, which I call the
prayer of quiet. Because of the great quietening it produces in all
the faculties the soul experiences the presence of God, it seems very
much at her will. This is true—yet sometimes, when the soul is
not so completely absorbed, one experiences it in another way. In
this sweetness it seems that the whole man, inward and outward, is
strengthened and comforted, as if a most sweet ointment were
poured into the very marrow of the soul, like a strong perfume,
as if we had suddenly entered into a dwelling where it was coming
not from one quarter alone but from many. Nor do we know what
it is nor whence that fragrance comes, but it pervades us through
and through.

4. This is what the Spouse says in my regard: 'Your breasts,
which give fragrance of themselves, are better than the best
ointments'.

5. She does not understand how, or in what way, that good
enters which she is anxious not to lose, she would wish not to move,
or even to look up, lest it should leave her. In another place I have
written what the soul has to do in this case in order to benefit by
it, and I only refer to it here that you may understand something
of what I am explaining. I do not want to say any more than that
in this friendship the Lord now shows the soul that he wants to
have such intimacy with her that nothing can separate them. Here
great truths are communicated to her, for this light is such that it
dazzles, because the soul cannot understand what it is, but it makes
her see and understand the vanity of the world, although she does
not see clearly the Master who is teaching her; but she is fully
aware that he is with her. She is so well taught and so much
strengthened in the virtues that afterwards she does not know
herself, nor want to do or say anything else but to praise the Lord.
When the soul is experiencing this joy, she is so penetrated through

and through with and absorbed in it that she seems to be beside herself with a kind of divine inebriation, so that she does not know what she wants or is asking for. In the end she is not conscious of herself, yet is not so much beyond self-awareness that she does not understand something of what is happening.

6. The truth is that when this exceedingly rich Bridegroom wants to enrich souls and delight them more, he draws them so strongly into himself that, like a person who swoons from great pleasure and happiness, it seems to the soul that she is held up in those divine arms and fastened to that sacred side and those divine breasts, and she can do nothing but rejoice, sustained with the divine milk with which her Bridegroom is nourishing her and making her grow in perfection so that he may be able to give her greater delight, and that each day she may merit more.

7. When she awakes from that sleep and from that celestial inebriation, she is, as it were, bewildered and amazed, and with a holy folly it seems to me that she can say these words: *Your breasts are better than wine.* For when she was first in that state of inebriation, it seemed to her that she could take no loftier flight; but when she found herself raised higher still and wholly penetrated by the immense greatness of God, she sees how she has been nourished and delicately compares this state to the breasts, saying: 'Your breasts are better than wine'. For just as a child does not understand how it grows and does not know that it takes milk, since without any seeking or act of its own they often put the nipple in its mouth —so is it here, where the soul of itself knows nothing, nor does anything, nor knows how, nor can understand from where this great good has come to it.

8. We should know that this is the greatest blessing that can be enjoyed in this life, even if all the delights and joys of the world were to be joined together. The soul finds herself nourished and led on to perfection without understanding how she can have deserved this. She has been taught great truths without seeing the Master who taught her, strengthened in the virtues, delighted by him who knows so well how to comfort and has the power to do so. She does not know to what to compare her blessedness, except to the delight of the mother who loves her child exceedingly and nourishes and comforts him.

9. Daughters, may our Lord give you to understand or, rather, to taste by experience (for in no other manner can it be understood) what is the joy of the soul when it is in that state. Let the worldly-wise come with their riches and overlordships, with their delights,

their honours and fine food and drink, for even if all could be enjoyed without the trials that it brings with it (which is impossible), in a thousand years it would not equal the happiness enjoyed in a single moment by a soul to whom the Lord comes in this way. If St. Paul says that 'all the troubles of the world are not worthy to be compared with the glory that we hope for',[1] I would say they are not worthy of, nor can they merit, one hour of this satisfaction which God now gives the soul, and no joy and delight can be compared with it, nor can the base things of the world ever merit a delight so lovingly bestowed by our Lord, a union so close, a love so expressively shown and experienced. Light are one's troubles in comparison with this! For if they are not borne for God, they are worth nothing; and if they are so borne, His Majesty metes them out to us well proportioned to our weakness, for, miserable and faint-hearted as we are, we fear them so much.

10. Christians! Daughters! Let us now, for the love of the Lord, awake from this sleep of the world, and let us consider that he does not even keep the reward of loving him until the other life, the recompense begins in this. Jesus! Would that I could make souls understand the advantage there is in throwing ourselves into the arms of this Lord of ours and making a pact with His Majesty, that 'I should look to my beloved and my beloved to me, and let him take care of my affairs and I of his!'[2] Let us not love ourselves so much that we blind ourselves, as they say. And again I would say, my God, and I beseech you by the blood of your Son, that you do me this mercy, that I may obtain that he 'kiss me with the kiss of his mouth,'[3] and that you give me your breasts, for without you, what am I, Lord? If I am not united with you, what am I worth? If I stray but a little away from your Majesty, where am I going to find myself? My Lord, my mercy and my good! What better do I want in this life than to be so joined to you that there is no division between you and me? With such company what can be difficult? What cannot be undertaken for you when you are so close? What have I to thank myself for, Lord—rather should I blame myself very much for my failure to serve you. And thus I beg you, with St. Augustine, in all sincerity, that you 'give me what you command and command me what you will', and by your favour and help I will never turn my back on you.

[1] Cf. Romans 8:18.
[2] Canticle of Canticles 2:16.
[3] Canticle of Canticles 1:1 [D].

GIVE US THIS DAY OUR DAILY BREAD
(from 'Seven Meditations on the Our Father')

These were originally ascribed to St. Teresa, since they were found among some papers belonging to her. Some of the homely touches would indeed seem to be characteristic. Authorities are now agreed, however, that differences of style make it impossible to accept the meditations as hers. They appear to have been written by a learned and spiritually-minded person of her time, whose identity so far remains unknown (see Allison Peers, *Complete Works of St. Teresa*, Introduction, p. xli). It would seem probable that they were written by someone who owed his or her spiritual formation to the saint.

1. The fourth petition is: 'Give us this day our daily bread.' Thursday[1] links up this fourth petition very well with the title of Shepherd, the one whose task it is to feed his flock, giving us daily bread; for Shepherd is a very fitting title for this Father, King and Bridegroom, and by natural right, we his sons and vassals and spouses can say to him that he should maintain and feed us, in conformity with his Majesty and our greatness, since we are his children; and therefore we do not say that he should lend this bread, but give it to us—and we do not say another's bread but our own, for since we are sons, our Father's goods are ours.

2. I cannot persuade myself that in this petition we are asking for something temporal—for the sustenance of bodily life, but for something spiritual—for the sustenance of the soul. For of the seven petitions that we make here, the first three are for God, the sanctification of his name, his kingdom, his will; and of the four that we make for ourselves this is the first, and in this alone do we ask that he should give; for in the others we ask that he should take away from us sins and temptations, and all evil. The only thing, then, that we ask our Father for, cannot surely be a temporal thing for the body—besides which, it is not fitting that sons of such a Father should ask for things so low and common that he gives them both to lower creatures and to man without their asking for them. His Majesty has especially told us that in praying to him we should seek first the things of his kingdom, that is, what concerns our souls, and of the rest his Majesty takes care; and therefore he said through St. Matthew, 'Give us this day our supersubstantial bread.' In this petition we are asking today for the bread of the

[1] The petitions of the Our Father are arranged each for a day of the week.

teaching of the Gospel, the virtues and the most holy Sacrament, and, finally, all that maintains and strengthens our souls for the sustaining of spiritual life.

3. Then let us consider this sovereign Father, King and Spouse as Shepherd, with the qualities of other shepherds and with all the immense additional benefits he himself sets out in the Gospel when he says: I am the good Shepherd and I lay down my life for my sheep. Thus we see how eminently the qualities of the perfect shepherd are to be found in Christ. Holy Scripture reminds us of this in the persons of Jacob and David. It says of David that, while yet a boy, he fought with bears and lions and broke their jaws to defend a lamb from them. Of Jacob it says that the sheep and goats he guarded were never sterile, that he never ate sheep or lamb from his flock nor failed to pay for any that the wolf ate or robbers stole from him; that the heat wearied him by day and the icy cold by night, and that he never slept by night nor rested by day, that he might give good account to his master, Laban, of his flocks.

4. It will be easy to take up the consideration at this point and apply these qualities to our divine Shepherd, who at such great cost to himself overthrew the lion of hell to pull away the prey from his mouth. When was any sheep in his care sterile? He guards them with loving solicitude; and when did he who laid down his life for them spare himself labour and toil? That which the wolf of hell devoured, he paid for with his blood. He never takes advantage of what can be gained from them: all that he gains is for them; and what he takes from them he has given them, as he has given them all they have. So much does he love his sheep that when one died he clothed himself in its very skin, lest he should overawe the others with the cloak of his Majesty.

5. Who can ever appreciate fully the food of heavenly doctrine with which he nourishes them? Or the grace of the virtues with which he strengthens them? Or the strength of the sacraments with which he sustains them? If a sheep goes astray to what is forbidden, he tries to draw her aside and bring her back with the sweet piping of his holy inspiration. If this does not succeed, he throws in her path the crook of some pain in such a way that he scares, but does not wound or kill her. The strong he sustains and makes to walk; he waits for the weak, the sick he cures, those who cannot walk he carries on his shoulders, bearing their weaknesses himself. When, after having been fed, they rest and digest the food and what they have grasped of the teaching of the Gospel, he guards their sleep, and seating himself in the midst of them with the

4

sweetness of his consolations, makes music in their souls, as the shepherd with his flute does for his sheep. In winter he seeks out sheltered places for them, where they can rest when weary, and guards them from poisonous herbs, warning them not to go near them. He takes them to the flowery places and pastures, keeping them safe with his counsel, even if they go through dust-storms and whirlwinds, or at times through ravines. As to the waters, he always takes them to the clearest and sweetest, for these signify doctrine which will always be clear and true.

6. St. John saw this divine Shepherd as a lamb in the midst of his sheep, ruling and governing them, guiding them through the freshest and most beautiful gardens, leading them to the fountains of the water of life. Oh what a sweet thing it is to see the Shepherd become a lamb! He is shepherd because he feeds, and lamb because he is that on which we feed. He is shepherd, for he sustains, and lamb, for he is food. Shepherd, because he rears his sheep, and lamb because he was born from them. When we ask him, then, that he should give us daily or supersubstantial bread, we are saying that the Shepherd is our food and our sustenance.

7. His Majesty is pleased when we contemplate him as he showed himself to one of his servants, in the guise of a Shepherd with a most sweet countenance, leaning on the cross as on a crook, calling some of his sheep and piping to others. It pleases him even more when we consider and look at him nailed to that same cross, as it were a lamb roasted and dressed for our food, delight and consolation. A sweet thing it is to see him carry this cross on his back like a lamb, and to see him carrying the lost sheep on his shoulders. As Shepherd he shelters us and receives us into his inmost heart, letting us enter there through the door of his wounds, and as lamb he encloses himself within our hearts. Let us consider how thriving, how sleek and how safe are the sheep who walk close to the shepherd, and let us try not to go away from ours, nor to lose sight of him, for the sheep who walk close to the shepherd are always the most favoured and he always gives them very special dainties from his own food. If the shepherd should hide himself or sleep, the sheep does not move from the place where he is until he appears or awakes, or until she herself, bleating perseveringly, awakens him, and then is caressed by him with some new delight.

8. Let the soul consider herself as in a pathless desert, in darkness and gloom, surrounded by wolves, lions and bears, without help from heaven or from earth, but only that of this Shepherd to defend and guide her. Similarly we very often find ourselves in darkness

and surrounded by ambition and self-love and by so many enemies, visible and invisible, where there is no other remedy but to call upon that divine Shepherd who alone can deliver us from such straits.

9. This is the day when we have to consider the mystery of the most holy Sacrament, the excellence of this food, which is the very substance of the Father, for David, extolling this favour given to men, says that the Lord fills us with the marrow of the inmost heart of God.

10. Even greater was this mercy than that of God becoming man; for in the Incarnation he deified only his soul and his flesh, uniting it with his person; but in this Sacrament God willed to deify all men, who are better nourished than with the food on which they were reared as children. As in baptism we were engendered from the whole of God, so he willed that we should be nourished from the whole of him, in conformity with the dignity he gave us as sons.

11. We have to consider the love with which he gives himself, for he orders that all should partake of him as food, under pain of death. His Majesty knew that many were to partake of him in mortal sin, but for all that, the love he bears us is so strong and effective that to enjoy the love with which his friends partake of him, he breaks through the difficulties and suffers these great injuries from his enemies. To show this love more, he willed to consecrate and institute this divine food at the time that he was delivered up to death for us. He willed, his flesh and precious blood being in either of the species, that each element should be consecrated separately, for in that division and separation he would show us that if it were necessary he would die for men as many times as the consecration takes place and Masses are said in the Church.

12. This love with which he gives himself to us, and the artifice that the divine love made use of here, is ineffable, because as two things cannot be united without a medium in which they participate, what did love do to achieve union with man? He took flesh of our clay, joining it with himself in the very Person of the life of God, and thus deified returns it to us, giving it as food to unite us with him through an earthly medium.

13. This love is what the Lord wants us to contemplate now when we communicate and here all our thoughts fall short. It is to this point that he wants us to come, and this is the gratitude he asks of us when he orders that in communicating we remember that he died for us. The eagerness with which he gives himself to us can be clearly seen, for he calls this food daily bread and wants us to

ask him for it each day; but heed must be paid to the purity and virtues that those who partake of him in this way should have.

14. When a great servant of his desired to communicate each day, our Lord showed her a most beautiful globe of crystal and said to her—'When you are like this crystal you will be able to do so'—but then he gave her permission for it. On this day we can meditate on the word which he spoke on the cross—I thirst; and on the bitter drink that they gave him, and the gentleness and sweetness with which the Lord nourishes us and gives us to drink can be compared with the bitterness with which we respond to his thirst and his desires.

The following 'Counsels' are written in manuscript on the back flyleaf of the 1590 printed edition of the works of Fray Tomás de Jesús (see p. 153 ff.). They bear no signature or date. Whilst their genuineness or otherwise must be left to experts to decide, the style would seem to suggest at least the strong possibility of Teresian authorship.

Whereas the 'Counsels' are described as being given to 'certain persons', after the first paragraph the pronoun is in the second person singular.

COUNSELS OF MY HOLY MOTHER, TERESA OF JESUS, WHICH SHE COMMUNICATED IN REVELATION AFTER HER DEATH TO CERTAIN PERSONS OF MY ORDER

May we in heaven and you on earth be one in purity and love, we in our rejoicing, you in your suffering. May the place of the divine Essence itself in all our actions here be taken, so far as your activities are concerned, by the most blessed Sacrament. This [counsel] I give to all my daughters.

Strive to arouse yourself and acquire the virtues which most pleased me when I was on earth—the chief ones were:

1. The presence of God, striving to do [good] works in the presence of Christ.

2. Persevering prayer, drawing from it the fruit of charity.

3. Obedience.

4. Deep humility, accompanied by shame at having offended God.

5. Purity of conscience, not consenting to deliberate sin, either mortal or venial.

6. Zeal for souls, trying to bring as many as you can to God.

7. Love of the most holy Sacrament of the altar, communicating with the greatest possible realization of what you are doing.

8. Special devotion to the Holy Spirit and to the Virgin Mary.

9. Patience and long-suffering in pains and troubles.

10. Transparency of soul and calmness of spirit joined with discretion and freedom.

11. Truth in speech, not speaking any lie or consenting that it should be spoken.

12. True love of God and one's neighbour, which is the summit of all perfection.

13. Strive to exercise the greatest attention possible at Mass and at the divine Office.

How small many faults and imperfections which people commit in life appear and how lightly we judge them, and how grave they are discovered to be and how differently God judges them, especially those which prevent an increase of charity.

Souls should not rely on visions and private revelations, nor consider that perfection consists in attaining to them, for although there are some genuine ones, many are false and deceitful, and the more they are sought after and esteemed, the more one goes astray from the faith, living charity, patience, humility and the keeping of the law, the way which God had laid down as most sure for our soul's justification.

I want my daughters continually to read the primer or catechism which contains the Christian teaching, meditating day and night on the law of the Lord.

When from some sweet feeling of the love of God or tenderness of spirit, there arises some rebellion of sensual nature, it does not come from God but from the devil. For the spirit of God is chaste and much familiarity between men and women is not good, for all are not like the Virgin Mary and St. Joseph, in whom familiarity caused greater purity, for they had Christ with them.

One should constantly speak against confessions badly made, for what the devil aspires to most in these times, and the cause for which most souls go to hell, is bad confessions, putting poison into their medicine.

To the convents which aim at greater poverty God will show greater mercies, both spiritual and temporal, and will give his spirit in double measure to those who practise poverty more.

So long as joy in God remains, the true spirit will remain in the soul, and it is not good to put pressure upon religious beyond what is ordered in their Rule and Constitutions. It is good to allow them a measure of innocent and holy recreation, so that they do not hanker after harmful ones.

The religious should give account of their state of soul to the prioress, in conformity with the constitution which requires them to do so each month, without hiding anything. This is of great importance for perfection, and when it is not done, the true spirit at which we are aiming will be lacking too.

The intensity of the desire to die which I had on earth, try to have in doing the will of God and not departing one iota from his commandments and your rule and constitutions; and strive after the virtues most pleasing to our Lord, which are purity, humility, obedience and love.

DIEGO DE ESTELLA
(1524–1578)

Diego de Estella was born in 1524 in the town whose name he bears, situated to the south-west of Pamplona. He was of noble blood, being a nephew of St. Francis Xavier. He was probably sent by his father to study at the university of Toulouse, later returning to Spain and continuing his studies at Salamanca, where he took the Franciscan habit.

In 1552, he accompanied Ruy Gómez de Silva, husband of the Princess of Éboli, to Portugal, where he seems to have remained for several years. A period of residence in Madrid, where he became adviser, theologian and preacher to Philip II, was followed by a return to Salamanca. It was he who, at the request of St. Teresa, preached at the opening of the second Carmelite convent there.

Diego wrote a number of works of spirituality, the ones for which he is best known being the *Tratado de la Vanidad del Mundo* ('Treatise on the Vanity of the World') and the *Meditaciones Devotísimas del Amor de Dios*, both published in Salamanca in 1576. The former is a work of asceticism, whereas the *Meditaciones* belongs to the literature of mysticism. An extract is here given from each of these works. The *Meditaciones* was a favourite book of Pascal and also of St. Francis de Sales, whose 'Treatise on the Love of God' owed much to them. Diego also wrote a life of St. John the Evangelist which contains, besides the biography of St. John, some teaching on contemplation.

Some of Diego's writings were censured by the Inquisition and before he was, so to speak, restored to favour as a writer, he died in Salamanca.

NO MAN CAN SERVE TWO MASTERS
(from *De la Vanidad del Mundo*, Pt. 3, Ch. 74)

No one can serve two masters, says our Saviour.[1] A heart has not room for two contrary loves and therefore it is proper that he who wants to serve God should despise and hate the works of the devil and the love of this world. Isaias says:[2] 'Too narrow a bed and one or the other must fall out; a short cloak is no covering for two.' If the love of the world dwells in you, there is no place into which the love of God can fit. If you cleanse your heart of the love of the world, you will enter into the divine love. He who has experience of God's consolation detests all that the world offers

---

[1] Matthew 6.   [2] Isaias 28:20.

to the senses. If men but knew the gift of God and knew by experience how kind and loving the Lord is and how pleasant it is to serve the King of heaven, with right good will would they despise all earthly things and the hard service of the world. To serve the flesh is death. It is to feed on worms, a food of diseases, corruption of the body, destruction of virtues, loss of goods and storehouse of many evils and sorrows. The service of God means bliss for the soul, health of body, prudence of the spirit and celestial life. Whom are you to serve, the Lord who treats his servants well, or the tyrant who ill-treats them? Christ commands things that are easy and the world those that are difficult. Christ sustains those who belong to him, the world puts its followers to death with hunger. Christ gives eternal life to those who serve him, the world throws [its servants] into hell. Which of these two Lords, then, is it right that you should serve? If you realize that you cannot serve both, for they order contrary things, there is no doubt that you should serve Jesus Christ and throw off the heavy yoke of the world.

He says you cannot *serve* these two masters. To serve God and *use* the world is a thing that is very possible, but to serve the world, making yourself its servant and slave, giving way to your appetites, and together with all this to serve God, is a thing impossible. Use this world as if you used it not, so that in using it you do good and do not become evil. Abraham, Lot, Job and David were good and perfect men, for they were not the servants of riches but made use of them. God wants the heart to be free and not a captive to the things of the world. The manna from heaven was not given to the children of Israel until the flour of Egypt came to an end and when the food from the earth was there to eat, the manna ceased. To those who want to serve two masters, the prophet Sophonias speaks on behalf of God saying:[1] 'I will destroy those who swear by Melchon and [also] swear by God.' You travel in two directions when you want to serve God and the world, like those whom the prophet Elias rebukes.

Leave, then, the service of the world and the dung of the earth for the food of heaven. If you have little inward consolation, it is because you seek outward comfort. We do not deserve to receive divine consolation, because we so easily accept human comfort when we ought to shrink from it with horror. Trees that have much leaf are shady and do not enjoy so much of the warmth and strength of the sun. You will not enjoy the warmth of Christ, the Sun of

[1] Cf. Sophonias 1:5.

Justice, nor the influence of heaven, if you serve the world and go cluttered with the whirling leaves of its business and green hopes— vain and swayed by every wind, as are the leaves of the trees and all the things you lay claim to. The shadow of vanity which you cast is an impediment which prevents the warmth of the love of God from reaching your heart. Leave the love of the world if you want the love of God to come into your soul. God and the world are contraries and so are the love of Jesus Christ and the love of this world. The love of Jesus Christ is a chariot of fire like that of Elias, drawing man up to heaven, and the love of the world is like the chariot of hell which carries men down to that place. Do not work at many things, try to serve one master only, Jesus Christ. Think of one thing and desire one good only, and you will find rest and ease. When Pharaoh gave the children of Israel leave to sacrifice to God in Egypt, Moses replied:[1] 'Have we perchance to sacrifice to our God the abominations of Egypt?' You cannot at the same time serve God and the devil. The Apostle says:[2] 'What is there in common between light and darkness? What harmony between Christ and Belial?' God and cupidity cannot dwell together. When Christ entered into the temple, he turned out the buyers and sellers. The heart cannot find room for two loves that are contrary. As fire and water cannot be joined, so you cannot love God at the same time as the world. Spiritual consolations are not given to those who love the good things of this world, wherefore if you seek temporal comfort, you will not enjoy heavenly consolation. A mother does not give milk to her child when he eats other food. You will be deprived of spiritual consolation if you regale yourself with that of earth. You will not enjoy God unless you despise the world for God, for God and the world cannot dwell together. The Lord your God you shall adore and him alone you shall serve, thrusting far from you the vain cares of this world.

Do not be busy about many things, for one thing only is sufficient for you. If the bee begins to suck from one flower, she does not go to another so long as she finds what she seeks in the flower on which she began, but continues until it is finished. Do not divide your attention in a variety of directions, you ought to be occupied solely with God, whom you began to serve, and to leave aside the anxious cares of this world. Ecclesiasticus says:[1] 'Do not be entangled, my son, in too many enterprises.' Distracted in many directions, you will not give your whole attention to one

---

[1] Cf. Exodus 8:26.   [2] II Corinthians 6:14.

single thing. In all you have begun, persevere, for if a man tries many different kinds of food, the result is disgust. If you enjoy God, serve him alone and do not go tasting nor trying the foods of the world, nor making continual changes. Leave the vain solicitude of the world to the children of the world. For you, Jesus Christ alone is sufficient, and with him you should content yourself. In earliest years and from childhood itself begin to serve God alone, for as the prophet Jeremias says: 'It is good for a man to bear the yoke from his youth up.' On the eighth day after his birth, our Redeemer willed to be circumcised to teach us that we should early begin to serve God, and to take the cross of penance upon our shoulders. As cloth which is dyed in the wool preserves its colour better than that which is dyed after it is woven and made up, so he who straightway in childhood and youth begins to serve God will have the habit of virtue implanted in him more deeply.

HOW ALL CREATED THINGS INVITE US TO THE LOVE OF THE CREATOR
(from 'Most devout Meditations on the Love of God')

Lord, all your creatures tell me I should love you, and in each one of them I can see a tongue which proclaims your goodness and majesty. The beauty of the heavens, the brightness of the sun and moon, the shining of the stars, the splendour of the planets, the running waters, the greenness of the fields, all the different flowers, the variety of colours and everything your divine hands fashioned, God of my heart and spouse of my soul, tell me that I should love you. Everything I see invites me to your love and reproves me when I do not love you. I cannot open my eyes without seeing preachers of your highest wisdom, nor can I open my ears without hearing heralds of your goodness: for all you have made, Lord, tells me who you are. All created things first show us the love of the Creator before they tell us of his gift.

Speaking of the creation of the world, the Scripture says that the spirit of the Lord hovered over the waters, as the most loving will of the craftsman moves over the mass of gold to draw out from it finished and perfect images: for we should understand that over all things hovered the divine love which sustains and governs them by a law of sweetness. Everything springs from the living fount of love and everything that has being is sheathed with love—in

¹ Ecclesiasticus 11 : 10.

such a way that if our soul's sight were not blinded with the baseness and dust of its own love and passion, the first thing it would see in everything created would be the love of the Creator.

All things stir you to the love of God: and they all, like an ambassador of their Lord, make you a request for love. The mighty sound sent up by all his creatures, both higher and lower, is an invitation to his love. This they audibly express, declaring to you his majesty, his beauty and his grandeur. 'The heavens tell forth your glory, O Lord, and the firmament declares the works of your hands: and there is no speech nor language where their voices may not be heard.' All the more, therefore, are all men without excuse.[1] Silently, Lord, the heavens manifest your glory and show forth what the dwelling of your chosen ones will be like, when you allow such great beauty to be seen by the eyes of mortals. How great are your riches, my God, since you make use of such rich lamps. From what primeval plan could such fine craftsmanship come forth? Who could fashion such glorious splendour and such variety of influences, movements so mighty and so varied, without erring in a single point? Rightly does Job inquire: 'Who can relate the order of the heavens and recount their movements?' Earth-bound heart of mine! How is it that the desire of seeing such great beauty and splendour does not bear you away to those celestial dwellings? Oh how great is the house of the Lord and how immense his dwelling-place! I see the heavens, the work of your fingers, and the moon and stars which you created. All that my eyes see tells me that I should love you.

If I turn to that lesser world which is man and set my eyes upon myself, here I find a greater reason for loving you. For all we have just mentioned you created for my service and profit. If I open my ears, I hear the psalmist saying to me: 'In myself I recognize your wonderful knowledge.'[2] From the knowledge of myself I came to the knowledge of your most high wisdom. It was for love of this that your prophet Isaias said to sinners: 'Return, transgressors, to the heart. In yourselves you will see who is your God.'[3]

[1] i.e. if they do not love God.
[2] Psalm 138. [3] Isaias 46:8.

LUIS DE LEÓN
(1527–1591)

Luis de León was born at Belmonte, in the province of Cuenca. His father was a lawyer and one of the royal counsellors. At the age of fourteen Luis went to Salamanca to begin his university studies; shortly afterwards he entered the Augustinian priory there. Melchior Cano was one of his professors.

His studies finished, Fray Luis was set to teach and later occupied in turn several chairs in the university. Always outspoken, he was denounced to the Inquisition[1] through envy and was imprisoned for over four years while his case was being investigated. In December 1576 he was released, cleared of every charge, and the story has it that when he again entered the lecture hall to resume his teaching, he opened his lecture with the words: '*Dicebamus hesterna die*'—'As we were saying yesterday'. In 1578 Fray Luis was nominated to the Commission for the reform of the Gregorian calendar. He was also concerned with the reform of the Carmelite Order and it was he who first edited and published the writings of St. Teresa, whom he greatly admired but never met. In 1591 he was elected Provincial of his Order in Castile, but died about ten days later.

Like the works of St. Teresa, Fray Luis de León's writings belong to the classical literature of the Golden Age. It is questionable whether he is not Spain's greatest lyric poet, though some authorities rank the verse of St. John of the Cross higher. His prose is gracious and elegant and its richness of vocabulary makes it not unworthy to be compared, in certain respects, with that of Cervantes. His output both in prose and poetry[2] was considerable. The works from which the present extracts are taken are: *La Perfecta Casada*—on perfection for the married woman, dedicated to Doña María Varela Osorio; *Los Nombres de Cristo*, a long treatise on the different names given to Christ in the Scriptures, and the *Cantar de los Cantares*, already mentioned in footnote 1.

[1] It is said that a nun had asked him to translate the Canticle of Canticles for her and that through the indiscretion of a servant, copies of the translation were made and distributed in contravention of a provision of the Council of Trent forbidding the distribution of the Scriptures in the vernacular.

[2] His poetry includes a metrical version of some twenty of the Psalms, and translations from Horace and other Latin poets.

ON EARLY RISING

'And she hath risen in the night and given a prey to her
household and victuals to her maidens.' Proverbs 31:15
(from *La Perfecta Casada*, 'The Perfect Wife', ch. vii)

The wife whom the Holy Spirit depicts for us here as the model
of the perfect married woman is, as we have said, the wife of a man
who earns his living by husbandry. The reason why a woman of
this particular type is given us as a pattern, we are also told. For,
as in households of this kind it is necessary for the family to get up
early in the morning to attend to their work outside in the fields,
not returning home until nightfall, so it is likewise necessary that
they should take with them what is needed for their midday and
evening meal, and that the portion necessary should be distributed
to each one in accordance with the work and tasks to which his
energies must be devoted that day; this being so, Solomon says that
his good house wife did not entrust this care to any of her servants,
while she remained idly in her bed luxuriating in morning slumbers;
but that she was the first to rise, stealing a march on the morning
star and being up and about before the sun, and herself prepared
for her household and family both what they were to do and what
they were to eat, not leaving this to other hands.

In this the Holy Spirit teaches and orders those who belong to
this state of life that this is how they should act, and those whose
circumstances are different that they should employ the same
watchfulness and diligence. Because, even if they have no workmen
or labourers to send to the fields, they have, each one in her condition and estate, other similar things relating to the daily and ordinary
good government of and provision for their household which
obliges them to wake and rise early and set their hand and their
attention to such matters. When these points have been generally
set down and understood, the Holy Spirit advises us of two things,
adding as it were two new shades of perfection and virtue to this
wife whose portrait he is sketching for us—the one is that she
should be an early riser; and the other that, rising early, she should
see, then and there, and personally, to what the good ordering of
her household requires. Both these things are of the utmost
importance.

'AS THE LILY AMONG THORNS'
(from *Cantar de los Cantares*, 'Canticle of Canticles')

'As the lily among thorns.'[1] Many times it can be seen that a good plant grows better surrounded with thorns or other weeds than if it is alone; this is borne out by experience. One reason for it is the natural appetite plants have for enjoying the sun, and another that the plants round about provide shade at its foot and keep it fresh and moist, and for that reason it grows better and more quickly. Besides this, the flower which springs up among thorns is all the more loved and valued, as the thorns among which it grows are more detestable; and from the ugliness of the one, the beauty of the other comes to be more clearly seen.

This being assumed to be the case, the spouse concurs in what the beloved says of herself, and adds that the rose can be seen and discovered more among the thorns than among other things; and in saying that, not only does he say that she is beautiful as a rose among others, but beautiful in the sense that she alone is beautiful and she alone is a rose, because the rest in comparison with her appear as thorns.

'DO NOT DESPISE ME IF I AM DARK ...'
(from 'Canticle of Canticles')

This is well in keeping with the nature of women who cannot take patiently anything that touches them in the matter of beauty, for, as it appears, this slight defect of colouring was well compensated for by the other graces that the bride declares were hers, although she will not speak of them again; but as it is a blemish, she tells us that this fault is not inherent and not of such a kind as to have no remedy, but has perchance come about through having been out in the sun, and even this not through her own fault, but forced against her will through the obstinacy of her brothers. Thus she adds: 'The sons of my mother strove angrily against me: they put me to guard the vines: my vineyard I have not kept.'[2] Where it says 'my vineyard', in the Hebrew the expression my *remia* has a twofold significance, giving us to understand how very much her own it is and how much she must take care of it, as if she had said: 'the cherished vine of my heart'; for in the opinion of women such

---

[1] Canticle of Canticles 2:2 [D].   [2] Canticle of Canticles 1:4 [D].

is all that touches their good appearance and elegance. She says, then, that she did not guard her vine, because she forgot herself and forgot about her face to attend to the other vines which her brothers forced her to look after. It is not to be understood that this was the case with the daughter of Pharaoh who speaks in this way, for since she is a king's daughter such a thing is not very likely, but it is to be assumed that the person whom she represents and imitates in her speech is a shepherd girl, and so it is the most plausible and kindly excuse and colouring she can lend to her bad complexion, to say that she has been out in the fields in the sun, forced by her brothers, who, being shepherds, were rough men and ill-disposed. In the underlying meaning it is very true to say that her brothers did her this violence, because no sort of people is more contrary to and a greater persecutor of true virtue than those who profess it merely in its external titles and appearances; and those who are in closest kinship with or under the greatest obligation to us, we often find to be our greatest enemies.

'I am black, but comely, daughters of Jerusalem, like the tents of Cedar, like the curtains of Solomon.'[1] This is clearly to be understood of Psalm 44, where the wedding of Solomon with the daughter of King Pharaoh is commemorated in detail.   As I have said, it is Pharaoh's daughter who here appears, speaking in the person of a shepherdess, and under the figure of the Church—she who was not so beautiful, as it appeared, from without, but rather in that which was hidden within, for it is said: 'The beauty of the king's daughter is within.'[2] Here then the bride answers possible objections from those who saw her so confident in the love of her spouse for her, yet at the same time seemingly dark and not so beautiful, always showing great modesty in this love of hers. She says, then: 'I confess that I am dark, but in every other respect I am comely and beautiful and worthy to be loved, because under this dark colour of mine great beauty lies hid.' She then shows the nature of this beauty by two comparisons: 'I am,' she says, 'like the tents of Cedar, and like the curtains of Solomon.' She calls the Arabs Cedar, because they are descendants of Adar, the second son of Ishmael, nomadic people who do not live in cities, but in the country, every year moving off to where they think best; because of this they always live in tents made of skins or canvas that can easily be moved. Thus the bride is beautiful in a very different way from what it appears, like the tents of the Arabs, which on

---

[1] *Ibid.*   [2] Psalm 44:14 [D].

the outside are black from the air and the sun to which they are
exposed, but enshrine within the many rich treasures and jewels of
their owners, and, like the curtains which Solomon was wont to
use in war, which on the outside were of skins for protection against
rain, but within of gold and silk and beautiful embroidery, such
as those of other kings are wont to be. This is as far as the letter is
concerned: for, according to the meaning which our Lord gives it
the inner sense is clear; it refers, namely, to the Church, that is, the
company of the just and whosoever among them appears dark and
ill-favoured externally, through the scant honour and respect, or
rather through the extreme ill-treatment, the world metes out to
them, so that it would appear that there is nothing more forsaken,
nothing poorer and more crushed than those who devote themselves
to goodness and virtue, yet they in truth are cherished and favoured
by God and full of incomparable beauty in their soul.

PRINCE OF PEACE
(from *De los Nombres de Cristo*, 'On the Names of Christ')

Even if reason did not prove it and it could not be understood
in any other way what a lovely thing peace is, this lovely vista of
the heavens which is now before our eyes, and the harmony which
those splendours which shine there from among themselves, give
us sufficient indication of it. For, what else is it but peace, or, at
least a perfect image of peace, that we now see in the heavens and
which comes before our eyes with so much delight. For if peace
is, as St. Augustine briefly and truly concludes, a tranquil order or
the possession of tranquillity and stability in what is required for
good order, that very thing is what this image now reveals to us.
There the starry host, set in orderly array and as it were harmonized
by the constellations, shines with utmost beauty. There each one
keeps its orbit inviolably. There none usurps the place of its
neighbour in its operation, still less does any, forgetful of its own
function, ever break the holy and eternal law which Providence set
for it; rather, like so many sisterhoods, as it were reflecting themselves each in the other, the greater communicating their light to
the lesser, they show each other love, and in a certain manner,
reverence, and at times in concert temper their radiance and their
strength, reducing them to one peaceful unity of power, composed
from the varied aspects of its parts, all-embracing and mighty above
all things.

If it can be thus expressed, they are not only a most clear and beautiful model of peace, but an announcement and a paean of praise that with clear and earnest voice declares to us how excellent is the good which peace contains within itself and which it operates in all things. This voice and announcement enters silently and swiftly into our souls, and from what it brings to them when it enters, its effectiveness and the force of its persuasion can be clearly seen and understood. Then, convinced of how lovely peace is and how useful to them, they begin to become pacified in themselves and to put each of their several departments in order. For if we are attentive to that which takes place in us in secret, we shall see that this harmony and order of the stars, when we consider it, puts tranquillity into our souls. We shall see, merely by keeping our eyes fixed on this attentively, without perceiving how our disturbed desires and longings, which in a confused manner noisily disturbed our hearts by day, gradually quieten down little by little, and lie dormant, as if falling asleep, that as each one takes its position and confines itself to its proper place, they unconsciously arrange themselves in subjection and harmony. We shall see further that, as they humble themselves and become silent, so that which is primary in the soul and is its master, namely reason, surges up and recovers its rightful place and its mastery and, as if nourished with this beautiful, heavenly vision, conceives lofty thoughts worthy of itself, and, in a certain manner, remembers its first origin and finally puts all that is vile and base in its place and tramples upon it. Thus when reason is placed upon her throne as sovereign and all the other parts of the soul are reduced to their proper spheres, the whole man remains ordered and in peace.

But what am I saying about us, that we are reasonable beings? This rough and insensitive world, the elements and the earth, and the air, and the brute creation, all put themselves in order and grow quiet immediately that resplendent host appears before them on the setting of the sun. Do you not see the silence that all things observe, and how it seems that beholding each other in this most beautiful mirror, they all grow quiet and make peace among themselves, returning to their proper spheres and functions and being content with them?

Peace is certainly the good of all things without exception and so, wherever they see it, they love it; and not only peace itself, but the mere sight of the image of peace makes them love it and enkindles their desire of being like to it, because everything tends easily and gently to its good. Yet if, as it is right to do, we acknowledge the truth, not only is peace loved in a general way by all, but it alone is loved and followed and striven after by all. For all that is done in this life by us who live in it and all that is desired and sought after, is to obtain this blessing of peace. This is the target to which all things direct their intention and the good to which they aspire. For if the merchant takes ship and sails the seas, it is to have peace with his cupidity which urges and goads him on. The tiller of the fields, in the sweat of his brow and breaking up of the earth, seeks peace, thrusting as far away as he can the harsh enemy of poverty. In the same way he who follows delight and he who longs after honour and he who cries aloud for revenge, and, finally, all men and all things seek peace in each and every one of their pursuits, for they are either seeking after some good which is lacking to them, or fleeing from some evil which is harassing them.

Because in this way both the good which they seek and the evil which they suffer or fear, the one with its desire and the other with its fear and pain, disturb the tranquillity of the soul and are as it were its enemies making war upon it, it may be clearly inferred that all that they do is done to avoid war and seek peace. If peace is thus a great and unique good, who can be the *Prince* of it, that is the author of it and its principal source, but he who is the principle and author of all good, Jesus Christ, our Lord and our God? For if peace is to be free from the evil which afflicts and desire which torments, and to enjoy restful tranquillity, only Christ makes souls free from fear and enriches them in such a way that there remains nothing for them to desire. But in order that this may be understood, it will be well for us to declare in order what peace is and what different manners of it there are, and if Christ is the prince and author of it in us, in all its parts and modes, and the form in which he is its author and *Prince*.

DIEGO DE YEPES
(1530–1614)

Fray Diego de Yepes, a Jeronymite friar, was confessor to King Philip II and bishop of Tarazona. The source of his *Historia particular de la Persecución de Inglaterra*, from which the present account has been taken, was the *Concertatio Ecclesiae Anglicanae* of John Bridgewater and others. Bridgewater based his work on Cardinal Allen's *Briefe Historie of twelve reverend Priests* (Rheims, 1582) and on the records at Rheims and Douai. The *Concertatio* was translated into Spanish, amplified and brought up to date by Yepes, who may well have had access also to the ambassador's correspondence. The full title of Yepes' work in English is: 'Detailed Account of the Persecution in England and of the most illustrious Martyrs there from the year of our Lord 1570 onwards'.

Fray Yepes also wrote the 'Life, Virtues and Miracles of the blessed virgin Teresa of Jesus' (Madrid, 1595), which was translated into French and Italian, as well as a monograph, written by order of Philip III, on the death of Philip II.

THE SPLENDID MARTYRDOM OF MARGARET WARDE,
A CATHOLIC SERVING MAID, AND OF A WATERMAN,
FOR HAVING GOT A PRIEST OUT OF THE PRISON
OF BRIDEWELL, IN LONDON, IN THE YEAR 1589
(from *Historia particular de la Persecución de Inglaterra*,
V, 2, fol. 614)

1. In the prison of Bridewell (notorious for the cruelty used against the Catholics there) in the year 1584, was imprisoned among others a priest of the Seminary of Rheims named Richard Watson, a god-fearing man, and one who had worked much in the Lord's vineyard; yet he was but a man and subject to frailty, so that on one occasion, after the tortures of flogging and the rack, and the hunger, and work beyond his strength, which they violently forced on him, such as grinding in a crushing-mill, beating hemp and other like tasks, he consented to go to the Protestant church.

2. As a result of this, although he obtained his liberty, he was more in captivity and tortured than before, for the blows that he suffered in his conscience after this sin were much more cruel than those he had before felt in his body. For the more cruelly they

tortured him before, the less he felt it, since he found himself
inwardly sustained by God who always gave him relief in the
sufferings men might inflict on him, but now he found himself
hated by men and deserted by the Lord who was his refuge and
comfort; heaven seemed to him of bronze and the earth of iron.
Both together, with all other creatures, threatened him on account
of his treason towards his Creator, while within there was the worm
of conscience gnawing him, and from that there was no place to
which to flee.

3. Seeing himself, then, in this wretched state, he went to one of
the gaols in London in which there were other priests imprisoned,
and with sobs and tears asked them for their advice. Finally, having
confessed and been absolved, that he might make satisfaction in the
very place where he had given scandal he returned to the church at
Bridewell, and when all were there together in their various functions, stood up in the midst of them and cried in a loud voice that
he had done much evil recently in having come, as if he were one
of them, to their assembly which was no service of God (as they
call it) but service of the devil. He wanted to say much more, but
all rose up against him, stopping his mouth so that he should not
speak, and each and every one having discharged his fury against
him, he was dragged off to prison and put in a dungeon so low and
narrow that he could not stand upright, nor stretch himself out
lengthwise to sleep. They loaded him with irons, and in their
meanness gave him bread and water in such scant measure that it was
barely sufficient to keep him alive. They treated him in this way
for a whole month, allowing no one to speak to him or console
him. But at the end of the month, not because they wished him any
good, but so that he might not die and end his wretchedness
quickly, they brought him into a cell less deep underground, where
at least he could see the sun and enjoy the light of day like other
mortals. They did not, however, fail to torment him daily with
threats, or to tempt him with entreaties and promises, so that he
should return to what he had begun or at least that he should
dissimulate and go to the church, although he believed differently
in his heart. They wore him out so much with this, that the poor
man wished they might end his life, rather than be forced to suffer
the vexations they were subjecting him to every day and hour.

4. The Catholics who lived outside in the town, on the other
hand, when they saw the suffering and misery in which he was
living, wept tears for him, although no one dared to come forward
and help him, lest he should be held to be an aider and abettor

of what he had done, until a serving-maid of manly courage offered her services to try to help him.

5. This maid, Margaret Warde, was servant to a lady of rank who at that time was residing in London. When Margaret heard of the distressing state of the poor priest, she was full of compassion, and asked leave of her mistress to interest herself in him. Leave being given, she changed her dress and, taking on her arm a little basket filled with provisions, went to the prison. When she had tried through other persons to get to where the prisoner was and failed to obtain what she wanted, she finally went to the gaoler's wife, begging her for the love of Christ to give her leave to go to the poor priest from time to time with some comforts, saying that he had neither father nor mother, nor any other friend in the city nor in the province to take care of him but herself alone and that she was in some sort a relation of his (meaning that he was her spiritual father) and that it would be on her conscience if he should die in prison for lack of the comfort which she could give him.

6. The gaoler's wife, then, partly through compassion, partly for the sake of gain, obtained her husband's consent to this, on condition that Margaret should be carefully searched on going in and on coming out, so that she should not bring in or take out letters. This was very strictly complied with for the space of a month, the bread and cakes and all she brought being broken into pieces to see if there were some letters or other thing which they might seize hold of, and while the girl spoke with the priest, there was always someone present to listen to her conversation. In the end they were persuaded that she only came to visit him through natural compassion for his condition. Accordingly, since they had searched so many times and found nothing, they began to cease to trouble about what she brought or about what she talked of with him, so that now from time to time he could speak some little word to let her know of his condition and what he wanted and desired.

7. When she had thus come to understand how the servant of God had found a possible way of escape from the prison over one part of the roof, one day she brought him in her basket, underneath the bread and other provisions, a long rope with which he could let himself down from the roof. She offered to send along two Catholic watermen, friends of hers, between two and three the following night, with a boat along the river Thames (which flows right by the prison) to take him away as he came down. So it was done. The watermen came at the hour appointed, but the priest, misjudging the height of the tower, doubled his rope, and attaching

it to one corner of the cornice, began to lower himself, holding the
two ends in his hand, intending when he reached the ground to
remove the rope and take it away with him, so as to leave no sign
as to where he had escaped: but when he had lowered himself
little more than half the distance, the rope came to an end, reaching
no further; thus he was suspended in the air, not being able to go
up or come down without danger to his life.

8. Finally, recommending himself to God, he let go of one of
the ends of the rope and thus came down with the other on to the
roof of an old shed which, with the weight of his body, fell to the
ground with a great clatter. The poor man was in a sorry state
with the fall, and his leg and right arm were broken. But the watermen came up straightway and before he could recover conscious-
ness, they carried him away and took him to their boat. As they
began to row away he came to, and, feeling the cold, remembered
that he had left his clothes where he fell. The watermen stopped,
one of them went back and fetched the clothes and they then proceeded on their way. But when they had almost crossed the river,
he mentioned the rope to them, saying that unless they returned to
remove it, the poor girl who had given it him would certainly be in
danger. Now, however, there was nothing to be done, for with the
clatter of the shed roof the gaoler had awakened and many of the
neighbours had hurried to the spot where, when they saw the rope,
they immediately suspected what had happened, and raised a great
hue and cry in the whole neighbourhood hunting for the priest.
The watermen, however, had put him in a place of tolerable safety
where, when his injuries had healed, he grew better. But in his
stead God took two others who suffered martyrdom on this occasion,
as will now be told.

9. When the gaoler saw the rope he realized (as was in truth the
case) that nobody could have given it the prisoner but the girl who
had access to him. He immediately sent to the house where she was,
threatening her with the law (for he had been careful earlier to
ascertain where she lived). Arriving there suddenly, they found her
already up and on the point of going away elsewhere; and so they
took her and with threats and much shouting carried her off to
prison, loading her with fetters and keeping her prisoner there for
the space of eight days.

10. Finally, they brought her before the court and there the
judge asked her if she were guilty of treason against the queen and
against the laws of the realm, in providing ways and means for
that prisoner to escape? She replied with a countenance full of joy

that it was so, and that through her whole life she had done nothing for which she was less sorry than for having rescued that lamb from the hands of bloodthirsty wolves.

11. With many threats and words calculated to strike terror, they tried to get out of her where the priest was, and not succeeding they condemned her to death for *lèse-majesté*. But they told her that the queen was merciful and that if she asked pardon of Her Majesty before those present and promised to go to church, they would set her free; but that if no, they would put her to death, in accordance with the laws of the realm.

12. She answered that she had done no wrong against the queen, and that therefore it was not right to confess it, asking pardon; rather, what she had done for that priest, the queen herself would have done if she had the heart of a woman, knowing how ill-treated he was. And as to going to their church, she said that for many years she had deemed that a bad thing, and that she could not so lightly change her opinion now nor act against her conscience: and therefore they were welcome to proceed to carry out their sentence—for it would afford her much consolation to give, if she had them, not one life alone but many to keep her conscience and her loyalty to God and his holy religion. Thereupon the judges, seeing that their words availed nothing, ordered her to be hanged. For this she thanked them much and went to meet death with joy, to the great edification of the people, leaving the hearts of all greatly touched by her example.

13. Whilst this was happening, the priest was hidden in the house of the waterman, recovering from his injuries, and when he grew stronger he tried to go elsewhere, and in order to travel more completely disguised, he changed clothes with the waterman, who put on the priest's garments with much devotion, but with scant prudence and circumspection. For as he went through the streets in this manner, the gaoler chanced one day to meet him and, recognizing the priest's dress, had him arrested forthwith: and forcing him before the justices to say where he had found that clothing, the waterman confessed the whole business, and as he replied to the requests to go to church and ask pardon of the queen in the same way that the girl had answered, he suffered the same martyrdom with much consolation for his soul and for many others who were edified and in admiration at his fortitude.

PEDRO MALÓN DE CHAIDE
(*c.* 1530–1589)

From Navarre like Bd. Alonso de Orozco and, like him, an Augustinian friar, Pedro Malón de Chaide was born in Cascante about 1530. Little or nothing is known of his early years, but in 1557 he made profession in the Augustinian priory at Salamanca, where he studied at the university under Guevara and Fray Luis de León. Later we hear of him as lecturer in theology at the Augustinian house at Burgos, and Professor of Sacred Scripture at Huesca. In 1583 he was given the Chair of Theology in Zaragoza, where he had earlier been prior. From Zaragoza he seems to have gone to Barcelona, in which priory he died in 1589. All his life he suffered from ill-health and so was prevented from making full use of his gifts for teaching and writing.

He is the author of one work—at least, only one work that is certainly his has come down to us—*La Conversión de la Magdalena*. It was immensely popular and the style is homely, direct and colourful. Its aim is to show how, like the Magdalene, the sinner should pass from the love of creatures to that of the Creator. The work was first published in Barcelona in 1588 by order of Malón de Chaide's superiors, as he himself relates in the preface.

OF MAGDALENE AT CHRIST'S FEET
(from *La Conversión de la Magdalena*)

Magdalene washed the feet of the Redeemer with her tears, wiped them with her hair, kissed and anointed them, and all this time not a word was heard from her lips, only her heart was melted in the fire of love. As green wood, if placed in the fire, when it is warmed on the one side begins to distil its moisture on the other; so, when divine love warmed that green and worldly heart of Magdalene's, the moisture began to flow out from her eyes in such abundance that *stans retro secus pedes*,[1] as she stood there, it was sufficient to water the feet of the Redeemer. And what followed was that, fainting away with love, she cast herself at the Saviour's feet. So, Mary, all has to be tears? Will you not say something? Will you not speak one word? Mary is silent. Only her eyes and heart speak. And will you not say something to her, Redeemer of life? Look

---

[1] Standing behind, at his feet.

how this woman of sorrow is becoming a fountain, like another
Biblis or Arethusa? See, Lord, those tears are now no longer of
water but of fire; see, it is the moisture of life which comes forth
from her eyes, and her very entrails, melted by the fire of love
which burns her breast, must almost come out too. God of goodness, do you want her life to end and her soul to take leave of her
body before you send her away from your feet?

O tears shed for God, how great your worth, how great your
power, how great your achievement! You achieve things which
seem humanly impossible. This is the water of the pool which
healed all diseases. But that water in Jerusalem healed only one
person; you heal all those who weep as they ought. What healed
Mary but the bath she made of such tears, with which she washed
the feet of Christ and cleansed the mire of her conscience?

JUAN DE LOS ÁNGELES
(1536–1609)

Juan de los Ángeles was born at a small village near Oropesa in the diocese of Ávila, probably in the year 1536. He studied Greek and Hebrew in the university of Alcalá, and then entered the Franciscan Order at Plasencia. He discharged various functions in the government of his Order, visiting Portugal, France and Italy. We hear of his being appointed Guardian of the house at Guadalajara in 1595 and later in Madrid. In 1601 he was elected provincial of the province of San José, but resigned after eighteen months of office to devote himself more fully to work for which he felt himself better fitted. After a prolonged period of ill-health, he died in Madrid in 1609.

Juan de los Ángeles' first book, the 'Triumphs of the Love of God', was published in 1589. He was already fifty-three. He wrote steadily from this time onwards. The 'Conquest of the Spiritual and Secret Kingdom of God' was published in Madrid in 1595. In 1600 came the 'Spiritual Conflict', an abbreviated version of the 'Triumphs', in 1604 a work on the Mass, in 1608, the 'Manual of Perfect Life'.

The 'Spiritual Conflict of Love' is a treatise on the love of God, with an analysis of the nature of love in general, God's love for man and man's for God. The work shows a deep knowledge of the ascetical and mystical literature of the Spain of his time. Both St. Teresa and St. John of the Cross are extensively quoted, as are Osuna, Alonso de Madrid, St. Peter of Alcántara and many others. Juan de los Ángeles made much use of the works of Fray Luis de León. Two extracts from the 'Spiritual Conflict' are given here.

OF TWO WAYS OF KNOWLEDGE, THAT OF WAYFARERS AND THAT OF THOSE WHO SEE FACE TO FACE
(from 'Spiritual Conflict of Love between God and the Soul')

There are two ways of knowing God, one through a mirror and dimly, the other face to face and as he is—and each has its due season. The one is that of pilgrims and wayfarers. The other is that of 'comprehenders'. The first is what we attain to during our exile. The second is enjoyed in the fatherland. Knowledge through a mirror is that which may be learnt about the Bridegroom through creatures, for, in a certain sense, their composition, harmony, order, beauty and grandeur, present, as it were, to the eyes of our intellect species of divine things, just as the mirror, when I look at myself in it, shows me and represents my face and figure. This is what St. Paul said: 'For the invisible things of him from the creation of the world are clearly seen, being understood by the things that are made. His eternal power also and divinity.'[1] The knowledge we have through the Faith is called enigmatic, because it sets divine things before us not openly, but with a certain obscurity, although with infallible certainty. It is so termed because the act of un-ravelling enigmas is an obscure science, and their true meaning can only be arrived at with difficulty. This may be seen in that saying of Samson: 'Out of the eater came food, and out of strength, sweetness.'[2] Also from what the prophet said in Psalm 86—'A man was born in her and he himself established her.'

This knowing the heavenly Bridegroom through a mirror and through enigmas is not direct knowledge but oblique, and ac-companied with a certain darkness: and this is proper to us who live in exile in this vale of tears. The knowledge the blessed in heaven have is direct and clear. They see God face to face and know his mysteries to the full. They have their eyes fixed on that divine Sun and do not blink or receive any harm to their sight. This St. John said in the clearest possible words—When our Redeemer Christ shall appear in the seat of Majesty (at the general resurrection of the dead), we shall be like him: that is, bright, subtle, light and impassible. We shall be like the iron which, entering into the forge, becomes red-hot sparks. It is iron as regards the substance, but its qualities and accidents are of fire. Those who reign with Christ, although they are not changed in so far as the substance is concerned, are changed in regard to their qualities which have become red-hot sparks. And, men as they are, they appear gods, for there they are many times more resplendent than the sun. We shall be like Christ (says St. John again), because we shall see God as he is, that is, we shall see him perfectly, we shall see him face to face, we shall see him in himself. The Apostle[3] made a distinction between our vision here below and the vision of the fatherland, as follows: 'Now I know in part, but then I shall know even as I am known';[4] as if he were to say more clearly— God knows me through his essence and I have to see and know him through that same essence: I shall see the essence through the essence.

---

[1] Romans 1:20 [D].   [2] Judges 14:14.
[3] i.e. St. Paul.   [4] I Corinthians 13:12 [D].

The *sicut* of St. Paul and the *sicuti* of St. John do not signify equality, as if there I am also to know God as God knows me, but unity of medium. Or, let us say, that to see God as he is is to see him immediately united to our understanding, not as we see the material things which we see with the eyes of the body. They cannot be seen in their immediacy, only through species or images, so that there is a medium—but God will unite himself to the understanding of the blessed without any medium. Thus we shall see him in himself and no longer in creatures. Now I can see light clearly in the air and in colours, but not in itself. In our exile we see God not in himself but in his works and effects, but *there*, as he is. There the desires of the saints who were always sighing and clamouring for this blessed vision will be fulfilled.

Some people try to reverse this order of seeing God, and the more they strain their eyes, so much the less light do they have, and the Bridegroom is displeased and goes far away from them. This appears to be what he meant when, speaking to the bride, he said to her: 'Turn away thy eyes from me, for they have made me flee away.'[1] While you are still in mortal flesh, do not strive to look at me, as those do who reign with me in glory, for I shall be displeased and go away from you. Content yourself with the knowledge you can attain to through creatures, who are, as it were, mirrors which represent me and give a certain knowledge, and with that which the Faith teaches you which is humble knowledge. For if you look at me directly, that is, if from curiosity and rash boldness you seek to see and know beyond that which is granted to your present state, then I shall flee away and withdraw from you. For this reason, St. Dionysius said that the mind of the contemplative was to have no eyes. At least we know for certain that one eye wounds God and it appears that two drive him away. St. Bonaventure says that this one eye is the affection which penetrates even to the deep secrets of God, whereas the hair represents the raising of the considerations of the mind.[2] I would say that the Holy Spirit is not here speaking of one eye, nor of one hair in the singular, but of one of the eyes and of one of the hairs. And if by the eyes we understand the affections and by the hair the thoughts (as all the interpreters of this passage understand it), that man who loves only one and thinks only of one thing[3] will wound and touch God, namely he who has all his desires and thoughts so simplified

---

1 Canticle of Canticles 6:4 [D].

2 Cf. Canticle of Canticles 4:9 etc.

3 i.e. God, as is apparent from what follows.

and united that none is apart from God. Thus that *in uno* means—
to my way of thinking—in unity, both of the eyes and of the hair.
Blessed is the soul who will not omit to attack, or cease from
attacking and wounding her Bridegroom many times with these
weapons of pure affection, considering that he will not move and
that she has him as a target for her arrows, for he receives such
wounds with favour, he who also knows how to inflict them.

OF THE GLANCE OF GOD AND THE WONDERFUL POWER OF HIS EYES, AND OF HIS FIRST TRIUMPH, WHICH IS TO INFLICT A WOUND ON THE SOUL
(from 'Spiritual Conflict', Pt. II, ch. 1)

Having discussed at sufficient length in the first part of this book
how our glance, when it is full of faith and charity, touches God,
reason demands that we should explain how we are wounded by the
glance of God. For it is not surprising that the loving glance of God
should wound, enrapture and delight our hearts, if our glance
causes these same effects in him. If against God love is strong, how
mighty will it not be against men? Great is the force of love (says
Richard[1]), great the power of charity, its degrees very different
from each other and who can distinguish them? And first and
foremost comes that burning and seraphic love which penetrates
the heart, inflames the will and pierces the soul itself with so much
tenderness that it can say to the Bridegroom what he himself has
said: You have wounded my heart, brother mine, you have wounded
my heart with one of your eyes and with one of your hairs. The
philosopher[2] said, and rightly, that where love is, there the eyes
follow. Thus when the soul sees the eyes of God turned lovingly
towards and resting upon her, let her ask whatever she will, for
she will receive whatever she asks.[3]

I will look upon you (God says to his people) and I will make you
to increase and multiply and I will confirm my friendship with you.
Abel esteemed it as a great favour that God should look upon him.
And when Cain knew that God neither looked at him nor accepted
his sacrifice, he was in despair, for it was on account of the death
of his brother. When God cast his eyes on the blessed Virgin, she
proclaimed that all good things had come to her. He looked (she

[1] i.e. Richard of St. Victor.
[2] i.e. Aristotle.
[3] The Spanish is obscure here—her mouth shall be (her) measure. The
above would seem to be the general sense.

says) at my lowliness and made me the greatest and most honoured of all women. I flourished under his glance and gave forth such fruit that on account of it I shall be blessed by all generations. That verse of Psalm 10 which says: 'The eyes of the Lord are upon the poor', is translated from the Hebrew which runs: 'The eyes of God are hidden in the poor.' By this the Holy Spirit means that as the rays of the sun, penetrating the earth and entering right into it, produce precious stones and the mines of silver and gold, and bring about other wonderful effects (for there is no tiny plant nor little bird nor any created thing to which its life-giving heat does not penetrate), so the eyes of God entering into the poor and humble, as the sun's rays do into the earth, create therein great wealth of virtue and heavenly riches. By merely looking upon St. Peter our Lord drew out of him the poison with which the infernal Basilisk had infected and slain him. With those eyes of his, he looked at St. Mark, he looked at the Magdalene, he looked at the good thief, and he looks every day at many sinners and makes them just and holy. Gently and lovingly he looks at his Bride, and as it were with an arrow flown from on high, he touches and wounds the heart with this glance.

Let us think (says Richard) how great is the depth of the love of Christ which he causes in the soul by his glance, and we shall see that it surpasses that of parents, wife and children, and, what is more, makes a man despise even his own life. Oh the intensity, the violence, the excellence and depth of the charity of God! This is what we are to discuss, not defining or arguing as in the schools, but humbly declaring its wonderful effects and its marvellous works, according to the opinion of spiritual and holy men. St. Bonaventure and Richard say that violent and heroic love (thus called not because it does away with free-will, but because with mighty power it carries away the soul so that it is enraptured with God) has four degrees. In the first there are wounds. In the second, imprisonments. In the third, sickness. In the fourth, failing of powers, and death. They mean that divine love wounds, makes sick, imprisons and even causes one's powers to fail, and slays. That love has the power of wounding souls is quite clear from what up to the present we have said of God, and from what the ancient philosophers commonly felt—for they painted love as a child, winged, blind, naked and laden with arrows, setting forth under this figure the passions and effects of love, both in those who love chastely, and in carnal and sensual persons. For this term 'love' is equivocal, referring equally to the divine and the human, to the spiritual and to that which is not so—although whenever we speak of love, especially in this treatise, we exclude all that is flesh and blood, for my intention is to treat of the love which God has for the soul and the soul for God. But we shall make use, for the understanding of pure love, of the things which the ancients said of that which was not pure— as the architect makes use of trestles and scaffolding to erect his building and construct his vaults, but when the building has reached completion, the scaffolding is thrown to the ground, so that the building may appear to full advantage.

We are saying, then, that love is a child, either because those who love are apt to be children in prudence, or because it reduces them to the simplicity and guilelessness of those of that age. This is clearly verified in divine love that brings men back to a state of innocence and makes them such that they can enter through the straight and narrow gate into the kingdom of God. Love has wings, for with the utmost fleetness do lovers present themselves before what is loved: and as Euripides says, they do not live in themselves but in what is loved; and also because love was never tardy nor backward in its workings. Of the creatures that Ezechiel saw, it is written that they moved backwards and forwards like a ray of lightning, which, as it sends forth fire, is neither heard nor seen. By this is meant that the saints who are on fire with the love of God are like fire in their operation—they go to God enraptured with his sweetness and return to their neighbours to remedy their needs moved by charity. In his Apocalypse St. John tells us of four living creatures around the throne of God who were full of eyes and who had wings, and who wearied not day or night in saying: Holy, Holy, Holy. The glorious Dionysius, explaining the properties of the seraphim (who are those most near to God), says that they love always, that they love unceasingly, that they love with ardour. All they can penetrate of God, they penetrate, and, like rays, they descend, through him, to the love of his creatures.

But why is love painted as blind? Because although it is founded on reason at the beginning, as it increases it is not ruled by reason. This St. Bernard well expressed when commenting on that passage of the Canticles where the Bride speaking to the Bridegroom says: 'Let him kiss me with the kiss of his mouth.'[1] Let nobody misinterpret this request nor judge as evil what the Bride has said through excess of love. For this is the voice of one who truly loves. 'They have given me more than I deserve, but less than I desire:

[1] Canticle of Canticles 1:1 [D].

I am carried away by desire and not by reason.' Blame no one for boldness if love reigns for, since it is vehement, it causes so many and such strange pains and anguishes in the soul that in no way can this passion be dissimulated or hidden. Perhaps it was for this reason that the Wise Man said—'Shall a man be able to hide fire in his bosom and his garments not burn?' What is love without fire, which of necessity must give sign of its presence wheresoever it may be, without reason or prudence sufficing to cover or conceal it? Plato found it impossible that this thing should be hid by him who ordinarily reveals so many things by his eyes, his voice, his countenance, his tongue, his sighs, his colour and other numberless accidents.

The glorious St. Bonaventure and Richard add to the external signs of love five internal ones, in their opinion most sure, and which they set forth and declare with moral certainty. These are deep and heavy sighs, high desires, sick thoughts, fastidious hopes, ecstatic affections. Each of these things requires explanation and comment, but because in discussing the degrees of intense love we have had to touch on this matter many times, so that there is sufficient knowledge of it, we will now pass under review the arrows which love carries in his quiver, with which he wounds not only men but also the gods.

ALONSO RODRÍGUEZ
(1538[1]–1616)

Alonso Rodríguez was one of the early Jesuits of Valladolid, his native city. He entered the Order in 1557, after studying Grammar and Philosophy at Valladolid and Theology in Salamanca. He later discharged the functions of Master of Novices and of Rector. From 1593 to 1597 he was teaching at the College of Montilla and in the following year was named inspector for Andalusia. He died in 1616.

His book on Christian Perfection (*Ejercicio de Perfección y de Virtudes cristianas*), written at Córdoba, which has become a spiritual classic in many countries, was published at Seville in 1609. It was translated into twenty-one languages, including Chinese and Hungarian. It is clear in style, written in simple but elegant Spanish and has a wealth of examples. Another work for which Rodríguez is justly famous is the 'Treatise on Conformity with the Will of God', published, after his death, in Tarragona in 1680.

OF THE IMPORTANCE OF SPIRITUAL READING, AND OF SOME WAYS OF PERFORMING IT WELL AND WITH PROFIT

(from *Ejercicio de Perfección y de Virtudes cristianas*, Pt. I, 5, ch. 28)

Reading is the sister of prayer and a great help to it. That is why the Apostle St. Paul advises his disciple Timothy[2] that he should give reading his attention. Spiritual reading is of such great importance for him who is trying to serve God that St. Athanasius says in an exhortation he makes to his religious: 'You will not see anyone who is really striving after his advancement who is not given to spiritual reading, and as to him who neglects it, the fact will soon be observable in his progress.' St. Jerome, in his letter to Eustochium, strongly recommends her to devote herself to this holy reading, saying: 'Take your sleep reading, and when, overcome by sleep, you begin to nod, let your head fall on the sacred

---

[1] This is the date given by Hurtado y Palencia, *Historia de la Literatura Española* (Madrid, 1943), and by the Espasa-Calpe *Encyclopedia*. Both Fr. Rickaby, S. J., in his translation of the work on Christian Perfection, and the *Catholic Encyclopedia*, give the date of birth as 1526.

[2] I Timothy 4:13.

book.' All the saints highly recommend spiritual reading and experience clearly shows how profitable it is, for history is full of great conversions which the Lord has wrought by this means.

It is because reading is such a fundamental and important means for our advancement that the founders of religious Orders, basing themselves on the teaching of the apostle and on the authority and experience of the saints, came to ordain that their religious should do some spiritual reading each day. Humbert (*Prologus*) says of the blessed St. Benedict that he ordered that each day there should be time set apart for this reading, ordering at the same time that at the hour for reading two of the most senior monks should go the round of the monastery seeing if anyone was neglecting or preventing the others from reading. From this will be seen how much store he set by it; and it will also be understood that the visits which it is customary to make in that Order each day during the spiritual exercises are based on the teaching and experience of the saints of old. The saint commanded that such a one[1] should be corrected gently for the first and second time; but that if he did not amend his ways they should correct him and give him penance in such a way that the rest should fear and take warning from it.

In the Society we have a rule about spiritual reading which says: 'All, twice each day, shall devote the time which is appointed to them to examining their conscience and to prayer, meditation and reading, with all diligence in the Lord'; and the superior and the prefect of spiritual matters take care that each one sets aside some time for this. Generally, of all the means which aim at virtue and perfection, this is one of those most commonly used; and thus, so that all may practise it with greater profit, we shall here speak of some things which will help towards it.

St. Ambrose, exhorting us that we should devote to prayer and spiritual reading all the time that we can, says:[2] 'Why do you not use the time when you have nothing to do for reading or for prayer? Why do you not go and visit Christ our Lord and speak with him and listen to him? For when we pray we speak with God, and when we read, we listen to God.' Let this then be the first means of deriving profit from spiritual reading, that we should advert to the fact that God is speaking to us and telling us what we read there.

St. Augustine[3] also has something to say about reading. 'When you read, you have to realize that it is God saying to you what you

---

[1] i.e. the monk who neglected, or prevented the others from, reading.
[2] *Officio*, 1, 1, c. 20.   [3] *Epist.* 143 *ad Demetriad. virginem.*

read, not only so that you may learn it, but that you may carry it out and put it into practice.' He adds another very good and pious consideration: 'Do you know,' he says,[1] 'how we have to read the Holy Scriptures? Like someone who reads letters which have come to him from his native land; to see what news we have from Heaven and what they tell us of our fatherland, where we have our parents and brethren and friends and acquaintances, and where we are wishing and longing to go.'

St. Gregory, discussing this, says[2] that reading the sacred Scripture, and the same may be understood of any other spiritual reading, is like placing a mirror before the eyes of the soul in order to see our inner life in it, for here we know and perceive the good and evil that is in us, and how much we are advancing towards or how far away we are from perfection. And sometimes the wonderful deeds of the saints are related to us there to encourage us to imitate them, and in order that, seeing their great victories and triumphs, we do not become faint-hearted in temptation and trials. At other times not only are their virtues related, but also their falls, so that with the former we may know what we have to imitate and with the second what we have to fear. Thus sometimes a man like Job is placed before us, who matured with temptation as yeast does in the dough, and at other times a man like David, who was overthrown by it, so that the former may encourage us and give us confidence in the midst of tribulations, and the latter make us humble and fearful in the midst of prosperity and consolation and never induce us to trust in or be certain of ourselves, but always to proceed with great caution and circumspection. Thus St. Augustine says:[3] 'That is the time when you make very good use of the sacred Scriptures, when you take them as a mirror in which your soul is reflected, trying to correct and remove from it the unsightliness and evil which is there reproved, and to adorn and beautify it with the examples and virtues of which you read.'

But coming down more to detail as to the way we have to follow in this matter, it should be noted that for this reading to be profitable, it must not be hastened or hurried, like someone reading a story, but must be performed with great tranquillity and attention. For as it is not swift-flowing water or heavy showers which soak through and fertilize the earth, but the soft gentle rain; so for reading to penetrate the heart and saturate it deeply, it is necessary

[1] *Sermo 56 ad frat. in eremo.*   [2] *Mor.*, 1:3, c. 1.
[3] *Epist.* 143 *ad virg. Demetriad.*

that it should be done with pauses and what we read be pondered over. And it is good, when we find some passage that stirs up devotion, to dwell on it a little more and make as it were a station there, thinking over what has been read, trying to move and stir the will, as we do in meditation, although in meditation that is done more slowly, lingering over things more and pondering and digesting them; but this should also be done, in a different way, in spiritual reading. This is what the saints advise,[1] saying that spiritual reading must be done as the hen drinks, for she drinks a little and then raises her head, and then drinks a little more, and lifts her head again.

In this it can be seen what a sister and friend reading is to prayer. So much so that, when we want to get someone to begin mental prayer and to persuade him to it gradually, thus appealing to the person's goodwill, we first advise him that he should read some books of devotion, in the course of the reading making his stations and pauses in the way we have explained, for through his so doing, the Lord is often wont to raise a man to mental prayer. Also in the case of others, when they cannot enter into prayer and it seems to them that they can do nothing therein, it is customary to advise them to take some book and join prayer with reading, reading a little and meditating and praying over it, and then a little more; for by this means, the understanding being thus riveted upon the words of what is read, there is not so much room for wandering off into all kinds of thoughts and imaginations, as when it is free and unattached. Thus in reading we can also make mental prayer.

This is the reason the saints recommend spiritual reading, praising it so much, and speaking of it almost as highly as prayer. They say that it is the spiritual food of the soul which makes it strong and firm against temptations; that it arouses good thoughts and desires of Heaven; that it gives light to the understanding; that it inflames and stirs our will; that it removes the sadness coming from the world and causes a true joy which is spiritual and according to God—and other like things.

The good St. Bernard gives another piece of advice to help us to profit by spiritual reading. He says:[2] 'He who comes to read seeks not so much knowledge as savour', and the pleasure of the will; for by itself, the knowledge of the intellect is a dry thing, if it is not applied to the will in such a manner that it feeds the heart

[1] St. Bernard, *Ad fratr. de Monte Dei*; *Spec. Monach.*; St. Ephrem, *Sermo* 7; St. Chrysostom, *Hom.* 20 *super Genesim*; St. Augustine, *Sermo* 38 *ad fratr. in erem.*
[2] *Specul. Monachor.*

and preserves devotion, which is what makes the reading fruitful and profitable and is the purpose of it. This is a very important piece of advice, because there is a great deal of difference between reading in order to know, and reading for one's profit; between reading to others, or to oneself. The first is study and the second spiritual reading. Thus, if when you read your mind is set on knowing things or in extracting what you can afterwards preach and say to others, that will be study for others, and not spiritual reading for your advancement. For that there are other times. 'All things have their season.'[1] The spiritual reading time is not for that, but for what we have said.

The saints[2] also recommend here for the same reason that one should not read much at one time nor get through many pages, in order that the spirit may not be wearied with excess of reading instead of being refreshed. This is another piece of advice very good and necessary for some, for it appears that some set their happiness in reading much and getting through many books. As the body is not nourished with much eating, but with the good digestion of what has been eaten, so neither is the soul nourished with much reading, but with pondering over and digesting well what is read.

For the same reason they also say that spiritual reading should not be about difficult, but about simple things, pious rather than difficult, because the difficult things are wont to tire and dry up devotion. Hugh of St. Victor[3] quotes the example of a servant of God who, by revelation, was warned that he should leave the reading of such high things and read the lives and martyrdoms of the saints and other simple and devout things, and so doing he made much progress.

St. Bernard further says:[4] 'Of what we read we must always retain something in the memory to ponder upon and digest better afterwards, especially what we see will help us most in our need, and that we may be thinking throughout the day on good and holy things, and not on what is useless and vain.' As we do not eat corporal food to waste the amount of time occupied in so doing, but that in the strength of that sustenance which we then take, we may be able to work all through the day and all our life; so, too, in reading, which is the food and spiritual sustenance of our soul, because what we read are the words of God, we not only spend well the time we give to it, but profit by it afterwards during the day.

---

[1] Ecclesiastes 3 : 1 [D].
[2] St. Bernard, *Ad fratres de Monte Dei*; St. Ephrem, *Sermo* 7.
[3] *Erudit. didascalicae* 1, 5, c. 7.   [4] *Ad fratres de Monte Dei.*

It will also be very good and will help us much in everything, if we raise the heart to God before we begin to read, and ask his grace that the reading may profit us and that what we read may penetrate and strike root in the heart, and that we may be left with a greater love of virtue and more clear-sighted and determined as regards what is necessary for us. Thus we read of the blessed St. Gregory that before reading he always prepared himself with prayer, and was wont to recite the verse: 'Depart from me, unclean spirits, and I will meditate upon the law and commandments of my God.'[1]

In order that we may value this reading more and find greater zest for it, the saints compare spiritual reading with hearing the word of God. They say that although reading has not the same power as the living voice, it has other convenient qualities which sermons lack. For, in the first place, one cannot have the preacher so much at hand, and that at any time, as one can a good book. Secondly, what is well said by a preacher passes into the air and thus cannot have so much influence on me; but what is well said in a book I can return to not only once but many times, ruminating and pondering it, and thus grasp it better. Thirdly, in the good book I have a counsellor who is both good and free, for, as the other philosopher[2] well said, what the friend or counsellor will sometimes not dare to tell me, the book tells me without fear, advising me of my vices and faults, scolding and exhorting me. Fourthly, in reading, I am conversing with those who wrote the book—sometimes you can go and have a short spell of conversation with St. Bernard, at others with St. Gregory, at others with St. Basil, at others with St. Chrysostom, and can be hearing and listening to what they tell you as you would if you had actually been their disciple. Thus it is said, and rightly so, that good books are a public treasure, by reason of the great riches and wealth that we can draw from them. Lastly, the benefits and good which come from spiritual reading are so great that St. Jerome, speaking of the interior fire of the soul, asks:[3] 'Where is this fire?' He answers: 'There is no doubt but that it is in the Sacred Scriptures, by the reading of which the soul is set aflame in God and becomes purified from all vices.' To prove this he brings forward what the disciples said when, as they were going to the village of Emmaus, Christ our Redeemer appeared to them in the guise of a pilgrim and was speaking to them of the Holy Scriptures: 'Was not our heart burning and on fire within us, when he was talking to us along the

---

[1] Cf. Psalm 118:115.   [2] Demetrius Falerius.
[3] *Epist. ad Damasum Papam.*

way and expounding the Scriptures to us?' (Cf. Luke 24:32) He also quotes that saying of the Prophet (Cf. Psalm 11:7) 'The words of the Lord are chaste and pure, as silver purified in the fire,' and St. Ambrose says:[1] 'Let sacred reading be the life of the soul, the Lord says (John 16:64): "The words that I have spoken to you are spirit and life."' For in order that we may live the spiritual life and walk always in the spirit on fire and aflame with the love of God, we should give ourselves in considerable measure to this sacred reading and make use of it in the manner we have explained.

From what has been said it follows that those people who when they have read some good book throw it into the corner saying 'I've finished with it now', do ill. A good book has not to be read once only—the second time you read it, you will derive more profit from it, and the third still more, and it will always be new to you. This is the experience of those who desire to advance. What some do is a very good practice, namely, when they find something in the book which moves them deeply and gives them special satisfaction, they note and mark it, in order to have at hand certain things of particular value in which they may more easily find some food for devotion or some comfort, at such times and occasions as offer themselves.

We might quote many examples in confirmation of the great good and advantages which result from reading, but I will only mention one, from St. Augustine, which contains much teaching. The saint relates[2] that when a gentleman from Africa, Ponticianus by name, came to visit him one day, he told him about the wonderful things which were said everywhere of the great St. Anthony, and he added further that one evening, when the emperor was in the city of Treves, occupied in watching certain public games which were being performed there, he (Ponticianus) with three other gentlemen of the court who were friends of his went out walking in the country. Two of them went off by themselves to visit the cell of a monk, and finding there a book in which was written the life of St. Anthony, one of them began to read from it and suddenly felt his heart burn with holy love. Angered with himself he said to his friend: 'Tell me, I ask you, what is it that we claim to achieve with all our labours, our long years of fighting in so many wars? Can we hope for more in the palace than to be the friends of the emperor? But in this condition of life what is there that is not insecure and full of dangers? And see through how many other

[1] *Sermo* 35.   [2] Confessions, l. 8, c. 6.

dangers we must pass to come to this greatest of perils. But if I want to be the friend of God, I can be so immediately.' Saying these words, in pain from the birth of his new life, he turned his eyes to the book and a change was wrought within him. He said farewell to worldly things, as was at once obvious; for after he had finished reading and his heart was disturbed like a ship tossed about in the midst of many waters, groaning heavily he said to his friend—'Now I am quiet and at rest. I have broken with those hopes of ours, and I am resolved to serve God. From now onwards I remain in this place; if you do not want to imitate me, do not try to hinder me.' The other replied that he could not be separated from him, nor do other than bear him company in the hope of such a great reward. Thus they both began to build up a spiritual edifice and follow Christ at full cost, namely, leaving all things. They were both married and, what is no less wonderful, their wives, when they learnt what had passed, consecrated themselves to God and made a vow of virginity. This is what St. Augustine relates and this example impressed him so much that he immediately broke out saying to a friend of his: 'What are we doing? What is this you have heard? The unlettered bestir themselves and bear away the kingdom of Heaven, and we with our learning are submerged in the deep.' With this change and deeply moved, the saint says that he went into a garden which was near by, and let himself fall at the foot of a fig tree. There, giving free rein to his tears, with great anguish and trouble of heart, he began to say: 'And you, Lord, how long, how long will you be angry? Is your wrath to have no end? Be not mindful, Lord, of our former evils.' He kept on repeating these words: How long, how long? Tomorrow, tomorrow. Why not now? Why not put an end to my slothfulness today? As he was saying this with deep feeling, he heard a voice saying to him: 'Take, read: take, read.' Then he says that he rose up to take a holy book, which he had near him, to read it; because he had heard about St. Anthony, that it was through a chance hearing of the Gospel—'Go and sell all thou hast, give it to the poor, and come and follow me, and thou shalt have treasure in Heaven,'[1] that he resolved to leave all things and follow Christ. He, then, moved by this example and still more so by the voice he heard, says that he took the book and began to read. There God poured into him such great light that he left all the things of the world and dedicated himself wholly to serving him.

[1] Matthew 19:21.

WHY WE SHOULD SERVE GOD WITH JOY
(from *Ejercicio de la Perfección y de Virtudes cristianas*, Pt. II, 6, ch. 2)

'Rejoice in the Lord always; again I say rejoice' and be glad, says the Apostle St. Paul (Philippians 4:4[D]). The prophet David repeats the same thing to us many times in the Psalms (Psalm 31:11): 'Be glad in the Lord and rejoice, ye just, and glory, all ye that are right of heart' (Psalm 69:5): 'Let all those who seek thee, O Lord, leap for joy and be glad in thee' (Psalm 99:2): 'Sing to God with jubilee, all ye dwellers upon earth, serve the Lord with joy: full of gladness come to his presence' (Psalm 104:3): 'Let the heart of those who seek the Lord be glad'—and in many other places we are exhorted to serve God with gladness. With these words the angel greeted Tobias (5:11): 'Joy be to thee always.' The blessed St. Francis was wont to say: 'To the devil and his associates it pertains to be sad, but to us always to rejoice in the Lord. "In the dwellings of the just the voice of gladness and of salvation should always be heard." The Lord has brought us to his house and chosen us among thousands: why then have we to go about gloomily?'

To realize that this matter is of great importance, it is sufficient to see how many times Sacred Scripture repeats and recommends it to us, and on the other hand to see the great evils which we said follow from sadness. But to treat the matter more fully and in order that, seeing the advantages with our own eyes, we may pursue it with greater zeal, we shall give some reasons why it is most fitting for us always to walk in the service of God with this joy of heart. The first is because the Lord wishes it. St. Paul says (II Corinthians 9:7): 'God loveth a cheerful giver,' in conformity with what He said through the Wise Man (Ecclesiasticus 35:11): 'Whatever you give, give it with a cheerful countenance.' Thus, as in the world we see that any great man wants his servants to serve him gladly, and when he sees them going about gloomily and serving him with sullenness and sadness, their service is not acceptable to him but rather makes him vexed, so it pleases God our Lord that we serve him with much goodwill and gladness, not with sullenness or gloom.

Sacred Scripture notes that the people of Israel offered much gold and silver and many precious stones for the building of the temple with great goodwill and gladness. And King David gave thanks to God to see the people offering their gifts with such great joy (I Paralipomenon 29:9). That is what God esteems highly. He does not esteem so much the work that is done, as the will with which it is done. Even here below we are wont to say: the will with which a man does a thing is worth more than everything, and that we esteem very highly even though the thing may be in itself small. On the other hand, however great it be, if it is not done with good will and joy we do not value it, nor are we grateful, rather it displeases us. It is well said that this is like someone serving good food but with bitter sauce which wholly destroys its taste.

The second reason is that to serve God with joy redounds much to his glory and honour, because in this way one shows that one is doing it with a very good will and that it all seems to us little in comparison with what we should like to do. It would seem that those who serve God with sadness wish it to be understood that they are doing a great deal, that they are breaking down under the load and that already they can hardly carry it, so large and heavy is it; this makes them discontented and it shows in their countenance. Thus one of the reasons for which the blessed St. Francis did not wish to see his friars with long faces, was because long faces show that there is heaviness in the will and lethargy in the body, in regard to doing good. But the others, as they go along light-hearted and gay, seem to be saying that what they are doing is nothing in comparison with what they desire and would like to do. As St. Bernard said[1]: 'Lord, what I do for you is scarcely the work of an hour; and if it is more, with love I do not feel it.' That gives our Lord great pleasure and thus he says in the Gospel (Matthew 6:16-18)—'When you fast, anoint your head and wash your face' (so that men may not see you are fasting). He means: put on festal garb and be gay, that it may appear you are not fasting or doing anything. 'Be not sad as the hypocrites', who seek to give everyone to understand that they are fasting, and who let it be perceived that they are doing something. It should, by the way, be pointed out here that there are some who think that to walk with modesty and recollection it is necessary to go about with head down and a gloomy face; they are mistaken. Pope St. Leo says:[2] 'The modesty of the religious person must not be a gloomy modesty, but holy.' The religious person should always show a happy modesty and a modest happiness. To know how to join these two things is a great asset and a great quality in a religious person.

[1] *Sermo* 14 *super Cant.*   [2] *Sermo* 4, *quadrages.*

The third reason not only redounds greatly to the honour of God, but also to the profit and edification of one's neighbour and to the enrichment of virtue. For those who serve God in this manner convince men by their example that in the path of virtue there is not that heaviness and difficulty which sinners imagine; for they see them travelling along it with so much joy and sweetness. By this those men who naturally like to be gay and happy are encouraged to give themselves to virtue. For this reason it is particularly fitting that we should conduct ourselves with joy in our ministry, since we are so much in contact with our neighbour and were instituted as an Order for the purpose of gaining souls for God. For in this manner many are won and become devoted, not only to virtue but to perfection and religious life. We know of some who have left the world and entered religion through seeing the joyful and happy way in which religious go about. For what men desire is to go through this life with happiness; and if they realized the happiness the good religious has, I think the world would become depopulated and all would betake themselves to religious life: but this is a hidden manna which God has hidden and kept for those whom he has decided to choose. The Lord revealed this hidden treasure to you and not to your brother, and thus he remained there and you were brought here—for which you owe God unending gratitude.

The fourth reason for which it is fitting that we should practise cheerfulness is because generally speaking a work is of greater value and merit when it is done with gladness and promptitude, for that makes us do the work better and more perfectly. Even of old Aristotle said:[1] 'The joy and pleasure with which the work is done is the cause of its being done with perfection; and the sadness with which the work is done of its being done badly.' Thus we see by experience that there is a great difference between him who does a thing with relish and him who does it with an ill will; for the latter, it would seem, is only concerned to be able to say that he did it; but the former is taking pains to do well what he does, and strives to do it to the best of his ability. We might add to this what St. Chrysostom says,[2] that cheerfulness and contentment of soul give strength and nourishment for labour. Joy enlarges and lifts up the heart, for the prophet says (Psalm 118:32): 'Lord, when thou gavest me that joy with which thou didst enlarge my heart, I ran with great fleetness along the way of thy commandments.' Then

[1] Lib. 10, *Ethic.*, caps. 4, 5.   [2] *Hom.* 41 *sup. Gen.*

the labour is not felt. 'They will run and not be wearied; they will walk and not faint' (Isaias 40:31).

On the contrary, sadness contracts, oppresses and cramps the heart. Not only does it take away the will to work, but also the strength, making burdensome to us what was before easy. Thus Aaron the priest confessed his weakness, for when, after the Lord had caused his two sons to die at the same time, he was reproached by his brother Moses for not having offered sacrifice to God, he answered (Leviticus 10:19): 'How could I please the Lord with my sacrifice, with a sad heart full of tears?' And in the Babylonian exile the children of Israel said (Psalm 136:4): 'How shall we sing the Lord's song in a strange land?' We see each day from experience that when we are in sadness, not only is our spiritual strength lowered, as the Wise Man says (Proverbs 15:13: 'With the sadness of the soul, the spirit is crushed'), but also our physical strength, for it seems to us that each arm and each foot weighs a hundred-weight. For this the saints advise that in temptations we should not become sad, for this takes away the strength of the heart and makes a man cowardly and faint-hearted.

From what has been said another reason may be gathered for which it is much to be desired that the servant of God and especially the religious should walk with gladness; and that is because when it is seen that a person is walking cheerfully in the things of virtue and religious life, it gives us great satisfaction and hope that such a man will persevere and go forward in what he has begun; but when we see him going about in sadness, we suspect and fear that he may not persevere. When you see someone carrying a great load of wood on his shoulders and walking with difficulty, panting and sighing, and here he stops and there a log falls off and further on another, you say: 'This man hasn't the strength for so much, I think he will have to leave it half way.' But when you see him going lightly with the load and he goes on his way singing and merry, then you say: 'This man could probably carry even more.' In the same way, then, when a man carries out the things of virtue and religious life, and it appears that he is groaning and breaking down under the burden, you suspect that he will not be able to last; for always to go rowing and forcing water upwards is the life of the galleys and a thing of much violence. But when he goes merrily along in the humble offices and other exercises of religious life, both corporal and spiritual, and all is done easily and lightly, it gives very good hope that he will go forward and persevere.

ST. JOHN OF THE CROSS
(1542–1591)

Juan de Yepes, known to history as St. John of the Cross, was born near Ávila in 1542, dying at Úbeda in 1591. He joined the Order of Calced Carmelites, found it not sufficiently austere and was thinking of passing to the Carthusians when he met St. Teresa. She persuaded him to wait, telling him of the project for the reform of the Carmelite friars and suggesting that God might be calling him to that particular work. As a result, Juan de Yepes became the first Discalced friar and undertook the reform of the houses of men.

Like those of St. Teresa, his writings—'The Dark Night of the Soul', 'The Ascent of Mount Carmel', 'The Spiritual Canticle', 'The Living Flame of Love', etc.—have become classics of Spanish literature. Professor Allison Peers' scholarly translation (1953)[1] of the works of St. John of the Cross is so well known as to make the task of selection for this anthology a difficult one. Intentionally, therefore, extracts have been taken from a minor work, the saint's 'Maxims', and the 'Counsels to a Religious on Perfection' have been given in toto.

St. John of the Cross with his doctrine of nada, nada, nada—nothingness, more nothingness and again nothingness—is often represented as an austere saint, somewhat aloof and unapproachable. A recent Spanish biography (1950)[2] by the late Padre Crisógono, O.C.D., has brought to light new material and, while the austerity is in no sense lessened, shows the saint to have been a very human person, tender to his sick novices, going to endless trouble and expense to procure the food best suited to them, and full of compassion for those who, while anxious to attain to sanctity, failed over and over again in their efforts to achieve it.

COUNSELS TO A RELIGIOUS ON THE ACQUIRING OF PERFECTION

In a few words your Holy Charity[3] asked me for a great deal, for which much time and paper would be necessary. As I find myself at a loss for both these things, I shall try to summarize, setting out only certain points or counsels which contain much in a short space.

[1] *Complete Works of St. John of the Cross*, ed. and translated by E. Allison Peers (Burns Oates, London, 1953).

[2] *Vida y Obras de San Juan de la Cruz*, por el R. P. Crisógono de Jesús, O.C.D. (*Biblioteca de Autores Cristianos*, Madrid, 1950).

[3] A title given in the Carmelite Order to religious who are not priests.

Whoever keeps these perfectly will attain to great perfection. Anyone who wants to be a true religious and comply with the obligations of the state he has promised God to follow, and to make progress in the virtues and enjoy the consolations and sweetness of the Holy Spirit, will be unable to do so if he does not most carefully strive to practise the four following counsels, namely: *resignation, mortification, practice of the virtues, bodily and spiritual solitude.*

To observe the *first*, which is *resignation*, he should so live in the monastery as if there were no other person living in it. Thus he should never intervene, either by thought or word, in the things which go on in the community, nor in those of private persons; he should not desire to know their blessings or their troubles, nor the kind of persons they are; and even though the world should come to grief, he should not want to take notice of or meddle in such things, or he will not preserve peace of soul. He should remember Lot's wife who, because she turned her head to attend to the clamour and noise made by those who were perishing, was turned into hard stone.

It is necessary to observe this with very great care, for thereby one will be freed from many sins and imperfections and will keep the peace and quiet of one's soul, with much progress before God and man.

And to this, which is so important, we should pay very great attention, for, through many religious failing to observe it, not only did the other works of virtue and religion which they performed never profit them, but they continually slipped backward, going from bad to worse.

To achieve and make progress in the second thing, which is *mortification*, it is important to set this truth firmly in one's heart —that one has come to the monastery for no other thing than to be exercised in virtue, and that one is like a stone which has to be polished and dressed before it is set in the building.

Thus, one has to realize that all those who are in the monastery are merely workmen whom God has placed there solely for exercising and polishing a man by mortification, and that some have to work on him in word, telling him what he would rather not hear; others by deeds, doing to him what he would rather not suffer; others by character, being troublesome to him and tiresome both in themselves and in their way of going on; others by thought, so that he feels or thinks that they do not esteem or love him.

He must suffer all these mortifications and troubles with interior patience, keeping silence for the love of God, realizing that he did not come to religion for anything else, but that they should work on him thus and he should be fit for heaven. For if it were not for this, there was no reason for him to come to religion, he should rather be in the world, seeking its consolation, honour, credit and ease.

This second piece of advice is quite indispensable to the religious if he is to fulfil the duties of his state and attain to true humility, interior quiet and joy in the Holy Spirit. If he does not practise it in this way, nor learn to be a religious, nor even what he came to religion for, nor knows how to seek Christ but only himself, he will not find peace in his soul, nor will he fail to sin and be often troubled.

For occasions of trial are never wanting in religion, nor does God will that they should be wanting, because, as he brings souls there to be tried and purified as gold is by the fire and by the hammer, it is fitting that there should not be wanting trials and temptations from men and devils, a fire of pain and discomfort. In such things the religious has to be exercised, trying always to bear them with patience and conformity with the will of God, and not to bear them in such a way that instead of winning God's approval in the trial, he should come to earn his censure for not having been willing to bear the cross of Christ with patience.

It is because many religious do not understand that they come to religion for this that they bear with others only with difficulty. Such men, when it comes to the time of reckoning, will find themselves put to shame and in great confusion.

To achieve the third thing, which is the *practice of virtues*, it is necessary to be constant in carrying out the observances of one's religious life and of obedience, without any respect to the world but only for God's sake. To do this without being deceived, a man must never allow his eyes to regard the pleasure or displeasure which the doing or omitting to do a particular work affords, but only the reason there is to do it for God's sake. Thus he has to do all things, pleasant or unpleasant, with the sole purpose of serving God by them.

In order to act with determination and with the constancy we have been speaking of, and that his virtues may come to fruition quickly, he must always take care to incline more to what is difficult than to what is easy, to what is rough rather than to what is smooth, and to what is painful and unpleasant in the work rather than to what is attractive and pleasing in it, and not to go choosing what is less of a cross; for the cross is a light burden, and the heavier the cross, the lighter it is, if borne for God.

He should also strive always for the brethren to be preferred to him in everything that is pleasant, putting himself always in the lowest place and that with all his heart; because this is the way to be greater in what is spiritual, as God tells us in his Gospel: 'He who humbles himself shall be exalted' (Luke 14:11).

To achieve the fourth thing, which is *solitude*, he should hold all things belonging to the world as over and done with, and thus when, because he cannot do otherwise, he has to concern himself with them, it will be with as much detachment as if they did not exist.

Of the things outside the monastery let him take no account, since God has withdrawn and set him apart from them. Business which he may be able to deal with through a third person, let him not do himself, for this is right and proper: that he should not wish to see or be seen by anyone.

Let him realize to the full that if from any one of the faithful God is to ask a strict account of an idle word, how much more will the religious, whose whole life and work is consecrated to God, be asked about such things on the day of reckoning?

I do not mean by this that he should fail to attend to the office he has, and to any other which obedience may send him, for neither God nor obedience requires that. He should do so with all the solicitude possible and necessary, in such a way that no blame attaches to him.

For this let him try to be continually in prayer, and let him not leave it even in the midst of bodily exercises. Whether he eats or whether he drinks, or speaks or deals with secular persons, or does some other thing, let him always do so desiring God and setting his heart on him, which is a very necessary thing for internal solitude in which the soul is required to have no thought which is not directed to God, and to be in forgetfulness of all the things which are, and which happen, in this short and wretched life.

In no way should he want to know anything unless it is how to serve God more and observe better the things he commands.

If Your Charity will observe these four things carefully, he will be perfect in a very short time, for they are inter-connected in such a way that if he fail in one, he will lose through his failure the gain and profit which he was deriving from the others.

SPIRITUAL MAXIMS—A SELECTION

(The 'Maxims' were collected from isolated notes written for the saint's penitents at different times.)

1. The Lord has always revealed the treasures of his wisdom and mind to men, but now that evil malice is uncovering its face more clearly, he does so in large measure.

2. O Lord, my God, who, seeking you with pure and single love, will fail to find you greatly to his desire and will?—for you make the advance and go out to meet those who desire you.

3. Although the way is plain and smooth for men of good will, he who walks therein will make little progress and that with difficulty if he has not good feet and courage and a firm confidence in what he intends.

4. It is better to bear a burden with the strong than to travel light with the weak. When you are burdened, you are joined with God who is your strength, and he is with those in tribulation. When you go lightly, you are joined only to yourself, that is, to your own weakness, for the virtue and strength of the soul increases and is confirmed in trials of patience.

5. He who wants to be alone, without the support of master and guide, will be like the tree which is alone in the fields without an owner, and which, however much fruit it has, passers-by gather it all and it will not come to maturity.

6. The tree which is cultivated and looked after with loving care by its owner gives fruit at the time that is expected of it.

7. The soul which has virtue but is alone without a master is like a lighted coal which is left to itself: it becomes colder rather than goes on burning.

9. Since you do not fear to fall alone, how do you presume to rise up again alone? You should think that two together can do more than one alone.

10. He who falls burdened will rise up again with difficulty with his burden.

12. God loves the lowest degree of purity of conscience more than all the works you can do.

13. God loves the lowest degree of obedience and subjection more than all those services you think to do him.

14. God loves your acceptance of dryness and suffering for his love more than all the consolations and spiritual visions and meditations you may have.

15. Deny your desires and you will find what your heart longs for; how do you know if your desire is according to God?

18. If it carries within itself the slightest desire of things of the world the soul has more impurity and less fitness for going to God than if it were loaded with all the ugly and troublesome temptations and darkness that can be named, provided that these are not admitted by its rational will. In the face of these the soul can confidently come to God to do the will of His Majesty, for he says: 'Come to me all you who are burdened and heavy laden, and I will refresh you' (Matthew 11:28).

19. The soul that in dryness and heaviness submits to reason is more pleasing to God than the one who, failing in this, does everything with consolation.

20. God is more pleased with one work done in secret, however small it is, which a man does not desire should be known, than with a thousand done with the intention that men should know of them. For he who works for God with the purest possible love not only sets no store by the fact that men may see his work—he does not even do such things that God himself may know. Even if God were never to know, such a man would not cease to render him the same services with the same joy and purity of love.

24. The fly who sticks in the honey is impeded in his flight. The soul who wants to be glued to sweetness of spirit impedes her liberty and contemplation.

25. Do not frequent the presence of creatures if you want to keep the image of God clear and single in your soul, but empty your spirit of them, withdrawing from them as far as you can, and move forward in the divine light, for God is wholly other than creatures.

27. The soul who is in love with God is a gentle, meek, humble and patient soul.

32. A single thought of man is worth more than the whole world; therefore God alone is worthy of it.

34. Consider that one's guardian angel does not always stir one's desire to act, though he always enlightens the reason. Therefore, to perform a work of virtue, do not wait for the inclination, since reason and understanding are enough for you.

42. Happy is the man who, leaving aside his taste and inclination, considers things in the light of reason and justice in order to carry them out.

53. As a man who drags a cart uphill, so the soul who does not shake off care and quieten the appetite, travels to God.

58. Take heed not to meddle in things which do not concern you, nor even allow them to pass through your mind, for perhaps you will not then be able to fulfil your own task.

59. Do not think that because in a certain person the virtues that you think should be there are not outstanding, he is not precious in the sight of God for things you have not thought of.

60. Man does not understand either how to rejoice aright or to grieve aright, for he does not understand the distance between good and evil.

62. Do not rejoice in temporal prosperity, for it is not certain that it will bring you eternal life.

63. In tribulation go straight to God with confidence, and you will be strengthened, enlightened and instructed.

64. In joys and pleasures go straight to God with fear and truth, and you will not be deceived nor entangled in vanity.

65. Take God for your spouse and friend, with whom you walk continually, and you will not sin but will learn to love, and necessary things will turn out prosperously for you.

66. If you forget them and yourself, you will rule people without trouble, and things will serve you.

67. Give yourself to rest, throwing away cares, and not concerning yourself at all with anything that happens, and you will serve God as he wills and rest in him.

68. Consider that God only reigns in a peaceful and disinterested soul.

69. Although you may do many things, if you do not learn to deny your will and bring it into subjection, dropping all care of yourself and your affairs, you will not make progress in perfection.

70. What does it profit you to give God one thing if he asks you for another? Consider what God wants and do it, for in this way you will satisfy your heart better than with what you are inclined to yourself.

71. How do you dare to take your ease so fearlessly when you have to appear before God to give account of the least word and thought?

72. Consider that many are called and few are chosen, and that if you do not look to yourself, your perdition is more certain than your amendment. The path that leads to eternal life is narrow.

73. Do not rejoice vainly, for you know how many sins you have committed; and you do not know how you stand with God. Fear, therefore, but with confidence.

74. Since at the hour of reckoning you will be sorry for not having employed this time in God's service, why do you not order and employ it now as you will wish to have done when you are dying?

76. If you desire to find peace and consolation for your soul and to serve God truly, do not content yourself with what you have left, because perhaps you will be hindered as much as before or more—rather leave all other things which remain to you and go apart to the one thing alone which brings all else with it, and that is holy solitude, accompanied with prayer and holy and divine reading, and there persevere in forgetfulness of all things; for if they are not incumbent upon you of obligation, you will please God more by learning to guard and perféct yourself than in gaining all other things together, for 'what doth it profit a man if he gain the whole world and suffer the loss of his own soul?' (Matthew 16:26 [D]).

JERÓNIMO GRACIÁN OF THE MOTHER OF GOD
(1545–1614)

Fray Jerónimo Gracián was born in Valladolid of a poor but very distinguished family. His father had been secretary to Charles V and two of his brothers discharged the same office for Philip II. He originally thought of becoming a Jesuit, but finally found his way to the Discalced Carmelites. Extremely gifted, all sorts of honours came to him at an early age, even in religion, to the detriment to some extent of his character. In high office he can hardly be said to have been successful. He was possessed of unfailing charm of manner and later events proved his fundamental holiness to be certainly genuine. He was St. Teresa's favourite disciple, her 'Paul', as she called him, though he did not come into her life until she was sixty. In her eyes he was perfect, yet the counsel he gave her was, to say the least of it, not always wise, as in the instance of the foundation at Salamanca. He was anxious to lighten to some extent the austerity of the life of the Discalced Carmelites, a policy which seemed to run counter to the purpose of their foundation. Like St. John of the Cross, though not at the same time, Gracián was imprisoned by the Calced friars in Toledo.

In 1592 Fray Jerónimo was unjustly dismissed from the Order and deprived of the habit by Doria's *Consulta*. On a journey to Rome to join the Discalced Augustinians, the only Order, apparently, willing to accept him, he was captured by the Turks and taken to Tunis. There he suffered torture and great hardships with the utmost fortitude. He was eventually ransomed and finally reached Rome, where he appealed to the Pope, who reinstated him in the Carmelite Order but among the Calced friars. After this he took no part in public affairs. He afterwards passed from Spain to Flanders, dying there in 1614 in the odour of sanctity.

It is to Gracián that we owe many of St. Teresa's writings, for it was he who commanded her to set down her life and experiences. His own literary output was considerable. Among his writings we may mention particularly 'The Burning Lamp', published in Lisbon in 1586, and the 'Pilgrimage of Anastasia' (1613). In this latter work he gives some account of his sufferings and persecution down to that year. It is very frank, but not entirely free from an attempt at self-justification. The short extract here given is from the 'Rule of the Virgin Mary'.

CH. 4 OF THE RULE OF THE VIRGIN MARY

Of the true spirit of the Virgin Mary which may be gathered from the canticle of the *Magnificat* in which it is set forth that he who would acquire a good spirit should strive to draw from prayer the fruit of esteem of God, spiritual joy, deep humility, gratitude for kindness received, fear, fervour and union with Christ.

Of the Esteem for and Magnifying of God

My soul magnifies God. In comparison with him, and with any and every thing belonging to his service, however small it be, it is as nothing and pays no attention to any greatness of this world, for when prayer is of true quality, the perfection of the knowledge of the divine excellencies and of the esteem of God arises.

Of Spiritual Joy

My spirit rejoices in God who is my salvation. If you want to please me, flee from the spirit of melancholy gloom which dries up the bones and rejoice again and again in the Lord, letting your modesty be known to men. For if you love God really well and reflect who he is, the eternal glory which he has and the infinite riches he possesses, you will not fail to attain to joy of spirit.

Of Humility

He who is mighty hath done great mercies to me and Christ Jesus, in his most holy name, as he crushes and resists the proud, raises up and gives grace to the lowly. Since, then, I was lowly and you desire to please me, hold yourself in the lowliest position you can, and desire and suffer insults for God. Exercise yourself in lowly works, love to be despised by the world and strive with all your might for true humility, asking for it in your prayers.

Of Gratitude

As ingratitude closes the gates of God's mercy and stops the hands of his magnificence and liberality, so the soul that gives thanks for the great favours which God has shown and does show to the world from generation to generation, and the special benefits which she herself has received, will receive great favours from God, for we cannot pay so great a debt to him with anything other than love and gratitude.

Of Fear

Fear is the beginning of wisdom which joins and nails our heart to that of Christ crucified, and God shows great favours to those who fear him with reverential, filial or even servile fear, and since he who fears God will do great good, if you wish to please me, try to attain to this fear.

Of Fervour

Those who hunger and thirst for justice and with fervent desires to serve God, the Lord fills to overflowing with his good things and theirs is the kingdom of heaven. They have sufficiency both in this life and in the other. Avoid, then, as much as you can, lukewarmness, coldness and laxity, and pray, love God and serve him with fervour.

Of Union with Christ

Israel received his Christ from the hand of the Eternal Father who sent him to the world remembering his mercy promised to Abraham and his descendants; and since this child, Christ, was received and born from my womb, if you want to please me greatly, try to imitate him and keep him present with you and unite yourself to him in true union.

ALONSO DE CABRERA
(1549–1598)

Alonso de Cabrera was born in Córdoba in 1549 (the year is disputed by some authorities) of a most distinguished family, the Godoy Cabrera. He received the Dominican habit in the priory of his native town and afterwards finished his studies in Salamanca. Later he proceeded to the degree of Master of Sacred Theology. After some years in the island of Santo Domingo where he became a preacher of note, he returned to Spain to teach philosophy and theology. He was given the Chair of Theology at the university of Osuna. It is interesting to note that, against St. Thomas, he held the doctrine of the Immaculate Conception of Our Lady. He was several times prior of his house.

Cabrera was one of Philip II's favourite preachers and it was fitting that he should be the one chosen to preach the King's funeral sermon. Not so eloquent as Luis de Granada, so vehement as Bd. John of Ávila, nor so polished as Luís de León, Cabrera yet surpasses them all in naturalness of expression, richness of vocabulary and freedom of style. He was gifted with a rich imagination and was a master of Castilian prose. Among his writings may be instanced the *Consideraciones Cuaresmales* ('Considerations for Lent'), a series of homely but polished *causeries*—a literary genre not common in Spain—and the *Tratado de los escrupulos y sus remedios* ('Treatise on Scruples and their Remedies'). The extract here given is from his *Consideraciones* on Our Lady, known as the *Soledades*.

CONSIDERATIONS ON THE LONELINESS AND SORROW OF THE MOST BLESSED VIRGIN, OUR LADY
Consideration II

Now we come to the loneliness of the blessed Virgin. After the Son's passion comes the Mother's com-passion, for you see how trouble pours upon trouble and suffering falls on countless sufferings already undergone, how reason was, as it were, turned topsy-turvy after she had heard from St. John and the Magdalene of the despatch and cruelty with which they were putting her Son to death and after she had gone forth to be an eye-witness of what was to cause so much sorrow to her heart. As the queen of Sheba who, hearing of the fame of Solomon, came from the ends of the earth to see for

herself his greatness and wisdom of which she had been told, after
she entered his house said to the King[1]: 'It is true what they told
me and I have seen with my own eyes even more than they could
tell me of your wisdom; they had not told me one half'—so at the
time when the true Solomon, Jesus Christ, was crowned with the
diadem of thorns which his mother the Synagogue put upon him,
and when he accepted the sceptre of the cross, and the government
was put upon his shoulder,[2] the Queen of Angels (the valiant
woman whose price is from afar and from the uttermost coasts)
when she heard the fame of his wisdom, came out, desiring to see
for herself what she had heard. Following right on to Calvary, she
saw the wisdom of Solomon, that cross of Jesus Christ which,
although it is a stumbling-block to the Jews and folly to the
Gentiles, is the power of God and the divine wisdom with which
he accomplished the repairing of the temple of the Church. She
saw the kingliness of his treatment, for frequently he changed his
garments. He changed them once in the house of Herod and two
or three times in the house of Pilate and they stripped him of them
once more at the foot of the cross, at much pain to his flesh. His
wounds, which opened and were torn afresh as the garments were
changed, began to bleed anew.

She saw the house which he built upon the cross, which is the
Church which he drew from his side, supported on the seven
columns of the seven sacraments, bedewed with the water and
blood which came out of the wound of his side. She saw the meats
on his table: all the affronts, insults, abuse which were the soups,
delicious meats and dainties on which he was to feed until he had
had his fill. As the prophet Jeremias says: 'He shall be filled with
indignities.' She saw the apartments of his servants, those caverns
and caves hammered out by force of iron in the living rock, which
is Christ, to make a dwelling for his faithful followers where he
invites the simple doves, that is, devout souls. 'My dove, come and
nest in the clefts of the rock and in the opening of the wall' (cf.
Canticle 2:14)—those five mortal wounds from which she saw
blood pouring down upon her.

Then she considered the order which was observed in serving
him and that although the ministers were violent, and blunderers
at that, they observed as much order as if they had the book of the
Sacred Scriptures before them. Some served him with insults, others
with blasphemies, others with different tastes and kinds of torture.

---

[1] Cf. III Kings 10:7. [2] Cf. Isaias 9:6.

She also saw the livery of the servants: not only the spears, arms, hammers, nails, pincers and ropes which the soldiers and executioners brought, but the livery and mourning garb which creatures brought out on that day—the sun darkened and the moon eclipsed to weep for the death of their Creator. She also saw the service of those who were offering the cup, noting that first they gave him wine mingled with myrrh to drink without his asking for it and afterwards, when he did ask for something to drink on the cross, they gave him gall and vinegar on a sponge.

Finally, she saw that sacrifice and holocaust of infinite value, burning there with all the fire of his cruel sufferings, offered to the Father and accepted with as much sweetness and willingness as the priest and the sacrifice of the old Law merited.

Then the royal queen talked with King Solomon of his secrets and riddles. Heart spoke to heart and the eyes of the mother met those of the son, the son who felt no wound more deeply than that caused by her presence. From the eyes of the son and from those of the mother, tears ran down which seemed like the four rivers of Paradise. Amid all her suffering, 'there stood by the cross of Jesus, his mother.[1]' Let her take her place in the body of the Church, namely, to be its neck.

Thus all the sorrows and sufferings of the son pierced the heart of the mother and wounded it more than if she had suffered them in her own flesh; it was then that the sharp knife that Simeon unsheathed passed through her soul: 'And thine own soul a sword shall pierce . . .' The sword of the passion of Christ pierced her soul and as she was standing right by the cross, the sword entered her heart right up to the cross [i.e. hilt]. From this St. Jerome concludes that the blessed Virgin was the greatest of all the martyrs, for they suffered in their sensitive flesh and Our Lady in her soul, which cannot suffer *physical* pain; they in what they loathed, their flesh, Our Lady in what was most dear to her, her son. The interconnection between the members of the body is so close that, as the Apostle says: '. . . If one member suffer anything, all the members suffer with it,'[2] and each one takes as his own the suffering of the other. What must have been the compassion, the anguish, the affliction of the blessed Virgin, who suffered such great pain in her heart and soul, that is, her son and her head? St. Jerome says that each blow they struck the Redeemer was a sword thrust for his mother. If then the body of Christ suffered six thousand stripes,

1 John 19:25 [D].   2 Cf. I Corinthians 12:26.

the head became a sieve of thorns, feet and hands were bored through and his whole body became a leprous wound, what must the heart of the Virgin have suffered? She is depicted pierced through with seven swords. Most loving Virgin, they should have depicted you with seven thousand, and that were all too little.

CRISTÓBAL DE FONSECA
c. 1550–1621

Cristóbal de Fonseca was born in a small village near Madrid, then in the diocese of Toledo, in which cathedral city he made profession in the Augustinian monastery in 1566. He would thus appear to have been eight or perhaps more years younger than Malón de Chaide. After his profession he disappeared from the public eye for about twenty-five years, but in 1591 he had become prior of the house of his Order at Segovia and in 1592 he was made 'Visitor' of the Province of Castile. His last years were spent in Madrid and he died there in 1621 in the Augustinian priory of San Felipe el Real.

His 'Treatise on the Love of God' appeared in 1592.[1] It was followed by a Life of our Lord. Fonseca's prose style won praise both from Lope de Vega and Cervantes and he was included by the Spanish Academy in its *Catálogo de Autoridades de la Lengua*. The 'Treatise on the Love of God' (which is a little unsystematic) treats of the love of man for God and the love of God for man. It then goes on to deal with particular vices and virtues. Fonseca's 'Life of Christ' is overburdened with quotation.

THAT GOD'S REVEALING HIS HEART TO MAN IS A GREAT PLEDGE OF HIS LOVE
(from 'Treatise on the Love of God', ch. 15)

Among the great pledges of God's love is that of his uncovering his breast and revealing the secrets of his heart, for friendship is the enemy of silence and reserve. Christ our Lord said this to his disciples: 'I have called you my friends because I have made known to you all my secrets.' And when God willed to destroy Sodom, it seemed to him that he would be doing a wrong to his friend Abraham if he did not let him know of that resolve. Can I, indeed, he said, conceal this from Abraham, when he is my friend?[2] Thus he called him out of his house and walked with him along the road to Sodom, and sent the angels on before, remaining alone with Abraham. Again, when Amos wanted to prove that all the evils which the children of Israel suffered were punishments from God, he said: This is a well-known truth, for before God sends such

---

[1] A second part of this treatise was published in Valencia in 1608.
[2] The Spanish here is obscure. The above seems to be the sense.

things, he reveals them to his friends the prophets. And he observes the law of friendship in this respect to such an extent that no punishment will come down from heaven without his friends on earth knowing it first.

St. Augustine says that there should not be silence among friends—he means that among friends there should be nothing secret or hidden, but they have to observe secrecy [in regard to other persons] and the secret must not go beyond the friends. One of the sayings of Pythagoras was that rings should not bear likenesses. And St. Cyril explaining this says that the great mysteries were only to be revealed to very few, for the light is not for bats nor the sun for the blind, nor, as the Lord says, precious stones for swinish animals, nor is the truth for liars, peace for those who are anxious and restless, learning for rustics, nor the things of the spirit for carnal minds.

Christ our Lord said: '*Eloi, Eloi*', which means, My God, My God. They said: 'He calleth on Elias.' He said: 'I thirst,' and it was thirst for souls and they gave him gall and vinegar. So that if they are not for his friends, his secrets are Arabic.[1] And in the psalm which says: 'God is the strength of those who fear him and he will manifest his testament to them,' St. Jerome translates: 'his secret'—'*Unde secretum meum mihi.*' From this St. Paul argues that God had more love for the Jewish people than for the Gentiles, for he confided many secrets to them. And David, judging this to be sovereign mercy and very great friendship, said: God did not give such friendship to any other people or nation in the world (Psalm 147). When God willed to speak with Moses on the top of Mount Sinai, he revealed to him secrets that were pledges of the closest friendship, saying to him—Let no one come up with you, no one hear us, with you alone I wish to deal; and in Leviticus he gave a similar command to the high priest when he was to enter into the sanctuary.

From this I infer that the understanding of Sacred Scripture, which is the book St. John saw sealed with seven seals, God gives with profit only to those whom he treats as great friends. This David said in a psalm: God gives good understanding of his law to him who keeps it (Psalm 110). He calls 'good understanding' the true and Catholic sense; this he will give either by divine inspiration, or through his Church, to those who keep his law, whom, elsewhere, he calls his friends. And Josue earlier said: 'Strive

[1] i.e. undecipherable.

to keep my law with all thy might and turn not aside from it even in a single point: I will give thee as reward, not only to find the true way but to know that thou hast found it.' He said the same to Solomon: 'Bend thy heart to true wisdom, and seek it as one who seeks gold when he digs the mine, for at each stroke of the spade he longs for it and it seems to him that he is finding it: as a reward for this labour you will obtain your desire.' And in the book of Wisdom Solomon again says that God manifests and reveals himself to those who have living faith, which is the same as saying those who keep his law. Through St. John, Christ our Lord said: He who keeps my law, he it is that loveth me and I will love him and reveal myself to him. Again, through Isaias God says that his prophecies will be like a book, sealed and closed for the Jews, by whom he meant all those who despised his law: for there is nothing that makes a man so blind as contempt for that law. Through St. Matthew Christ our Lord said that this secret of which we are talking was a hidden treasure, and as they who find the treasure are few, and the finding is more by chance than by diligence, so they are few to whom God reveals his secret, and then more by grace and friendship than by their own deserts. God gives them the eyes of the lynx and makes diviners of heaven those who discern the treasure there is in poverty, in tears, in contempt of the world, in suffering insults and persecutions.

This is the purpose God had in speaking in parables and as he finished preaching the one about the sower his disciples objected: 'Lord, either you want these people to understand you or not to understand you, but if you do not want them to understand you, do not preach to them, and if you want them to understand you, why these parables and these enigmas?' The Lord answered: 'To you high heaven grants that you understand these secrets, for God has his friends and favourites for whom there is nothing kept separate or hidden: but to the rest in parables, that seeing they may not see and hearing they may not understand. In this the disciples did not ask him why he generally spoke in parables, but why he had spoken in parables on that occasion, and he answered thus: 'I do not will to show to these the friendship I have for you and if anyone should ask me how it is that in the Sermon on the Mount I preached a plain doctrine to all indiscriminately without saying anything which might seem a parable—I reply that there I was giving the precepts of the Gospel, which no one should be ignorant of, but here I treat of heavenly mysteries and, thus said the Lord, there is no reason for them to be revealed to all but only to friends.

When the son of the widow who had given hospitality to Eliseus died, the prophet was dismayed, not so much at the death of the boy as that God had hidden it from him. He laid claim to such great friendship that it seemed to him that God would not do a thing so contrary to his desires without telling him of it; and thus he said as if astounded: God hath hidden it from me. Delilah in her anxiety claimed that Samson loved her so little that he would not reveal the secret of his strength to her, and she continued to coax with diligence and skill until, seeing herself three times mocked, she burst into anger against her husband and said to him: How can you say you love me when you hide your heart and soul from me?

Thus it is sufficiently proved that God's revealing his secrets to us is a pledge of divine love. Thus Osee promises his people as a singular favour: I will take thee out from the tumult of Babylon and carry thee into solitude and there I will speak to thy heart: he means, I will reveal great things to thee—according to that saying of Isaias: *Loquimini ad cor Jerusalem.*

FRANCISCO DE QUEVEDO
(1580–1645)

Francisco Gómez de Quevedo y Villegas was born in Madrid. His family, a distinguished one, came from near Burgos. His father was secretary, first to Doña María de Austria (sister of Philip II) whom he accompanied into Germany, and later to the Queen, Doña Ana of Austria. Quevedo was brought up at the court, his mother being in the service of the Infanta Isabel Clara Eugenia. In due course he entered the university of Alcalá de Henares, reading Classics. He seems to have rivalled Pascal in his learning, for he had a knowledge not only of mathematics and astronomy, but of civil and canon law, Arabic, French, Italian and Hebrew. He also graduated in theology.

With the vicissitudes of Quevedo's life in the service of the Duke of Osuna, his diplomatic missions, his exile and imprisonment, we are not here concerned. He is chiefly known as poet and satirist, but, a fervent Catholic and a man of lively faith, he also wrote a number of religious works, among which we may instance the lives of St. Paul and of St. Thomas of Villanueva, and a book on the Providence of God. He translated St. Francis of Sales' 'Introduction to the Devout Life' (then, of course, a recent work) into Spanish. The extract here given is from his life of St. Paul the Apostle.

ST. PAUL'S CONVERSION
(from *La Vida de San Pablo*)

Let us listen to the canonical account of the event: 'And as Paul was going on his way to reach Damascus, suddenly, dazzled by the brightness of light which came down from heaven, he fell to the ground; and he heard a voice which said to him: Saul, Saul, why persecutest thou me?'[1]

Many of God's edifices begin by being overthrown and are founded on a ruin. The world raises up to cast down, God casts down in order to raise up. Paul alone was baffled by the abundance of light and, though blinded, was flooded with brightness—a rich promise, bathed in light, which would flow through the world as the light of day and most magnificent substitute for the sun, to enlighten the Gentiles. He heard a voice which called him twice

[1] Cf. Acts 9.

148

by name. When this repetition fell on his ears, it sounded like a
caress. 'Saul, Saul, why persecutest thou me?' He answered: 'Who
art thou, Lord?' He said to him: 'I am Jesus whom thou persecutest;
in vain thou resistest my calls.' He, trembling and pondering, said:
'Lord, what wilt thou have me to do?' He remarks especially that
Christ asks him why he persecutes him; for he realizes that this is
Jesus himself (as indeed it is—he gives his name) who must know
that he, Paul, as a Pharisee does not believe him to be the anointed
one nor the Messias who is called Christ. But this is not the point
—the question was both mysterious and legitimate; it was at one
and the same time a question and a charge. God, who knows all,
does not ask in order to know what he asks, but that man may
know it. This was the case with Adam and with Cain.

I shall unfold something of the implications of the question.
Paul had heard that Christ had risen on the third day. He had just
been listening to Stephen who saw the Lord in glory at his Father's
side, and the same Lord says to him: 'Saul, why persecutest thou
me, since thou canst no longer lay thy hands on me, since the nails
and hammers cannot touch me, since the injuries inflicted by men
such as thyself have now given place to triumphant majesty and the
wounds are so many shining stars which scintillate light on the
humanity of my body. It is due to my grace that it has been reserved
to thee to be the artificer of my passion which I have undergone to
convert thee, and which thou seest exemplified in my first witness,
that is, proto-martyr. In the midst of those who were stoning him,
thou heardest him pray to me for thee, and I am casting thee to the
ground so that thou mayst see that I have heard him in thy favour.
Why, then, obstinate to so many calls, and heedless of so many
benefits, and of a favour so great as for me to call thee to my service
from the glory of heaven and the right hand of my Father, dost
thou persecute me?' It seems that Paul immediately fell to the
ground at Christ's words in fear and bewilderment; he replied:
'Lord, what wilt thou have me to do?' Now to tremble is to
recognize one's guilt; to call lord him who is overthrowing one
and blinding one is to surrender reverently to the punishment as
just. Paul has left us a great lesson as to what we should do when the
Lord sends us trials as a warning. He did not wait to rise or to
recover his sight to begin to teach and be a master: he calls him lord
who casts him down and darkens his sight; he does not ask him
to give back the use of his eyes, nor that he should raise him up
from the ground and take away his fear; he only asks that the Lord
should tell him what to do to be in conformity with his will.

6

This was to forget his own will for that of God: never was divine rhetoric found epitomized in fewer words. Paul prayed in a single phrase, teaching us that when God visits us by trials, it is on account of whatever we are doing by our own will, and that the remedy is to ask him to teach us what we have to do according to his will. What Paul obtained by this was that the Lord said to him: 'Arise and go into the city and there it shall be told thee what thou hast to do.' The men who were with him and travelling in his company were amazed at hearing the voice without seeing him who uttered the words or anyone else.

Christ ordered him, fallen and dumbfounded as he was, to rise; he had the power to command those who were with him that they should help him to get up. He blinded him and ordered him who could not see the way to enter into the city. 'Paul straightway rose from the ground, and when his eyes were opened he could not see.'

In such a way and with such promptitude and with blind eyes, as they say, God must be obeyed, without heeding the physical impediment or what man lacks in himself, [but] expecting all from the commandment of God. 'Leading him by the hand, his companions took him into Damascus, where he was blind for three days, neither eating nor drinking.' They took him to Damascus trembling and stricken by blindness, for his salvation, [leading] by the hand him who had intended to drag to their death from Damascus to Jerusalem, trembling and with hands bound, the Christians who were now to give him sight.

Paul doubtless pondered over the circumstances of this event, so different from what he had expected, for instead of having recourse to physicians for his eyes, he chose penance as an eyesalve and fasted for a space of three days: 'There was in Damascus a certain disciple called Ananias and the Lord said to him in a vision: "Ananias." He replied: "Lord, here I am." The Lord said to him again: "Arise and go to the street that is called Straight and inquire in the house of Juda for Saul of Tarsus; for even now when he was in prayer, he saw a man called Ananias, who went into him and touched him with his hands that he might receive his sight."'

Christ took away Paul's sight, he who cast him to the ground bade him arise; and, though he had the power to restore his sight, he handed him over to be touched by Ananias, his servant. He first brought it about that Paul should see Ananias healing him in vision; then he related Paul's vision to Ananias and told him to go and give him sight. And what seems a detour and a long way round is really an epitome and compendium of manifold mercies. What else could happen to Paul, who upon receiving the chastisement of God, betook himself to fasting and gave himself over to prayer? From which it can be known that he who blinded his bodily eyes, since he sent him to Ananias to restore them, opened and gave sight to those of the soul. There are many miracles which God refrains from working, leaving them to his servants to perform, to honour them, and that by such miracles they may glorify him. Let Paul be restored to health by him who was expecting death from his persecution; let him see, at the same time as he receives his sight, how the disciples of Jesus fulfil his precept to love their enemies in the person of him who was the greatest enemy. This was the teaching he had begun to hear from Stephen, when with his last words and the last drop of his blood, he asked pardon for him among those who were stoning him; and he sees it exemplified in Ananias whom he had come to arrest and who, with all the Christians of Damascus, trembled at his name.

I will illustrate from Paul how excellent prayer and fasting are for fashioning unto Christ his chosen vessels. 'Ananias answered: "Lord, I have heard many things of this man and how much evil he has wrought in Jerusalem to thy saints; and he has power from the chief priests to seize all those who invoke thy name." The Lord answered him: "Behold he is to me a vessel of election to carry my name before the Gentiles and before the kings and children of Israel; I will show him what great things he must suffer for my name."'

How difficult it is to thrust aside the notion of Paul as a persecutor of goodness may be realized from the fact that when Christ told Ananias that Paul was at prayer and that he had revealed to him that Ananias would heal him and ordered him to go and restore his sight, he replies saying that he had heard the evils that Paul has wrought, persecuting his saints in Jerusalem, and that he is bringing with him the commission to persecute all those who invoke Christ's name. The righteous fear of Ananias moves God to strengthen his confidence by saying that Paul, who was an offensive weapon against him (that is what 'vessel' means in Holy Scripture), was to be his weapon of election for the defence of his law; and that he would carry his name, which he had persecuted, to all the Gentiles, preaching it to the kings and children of Israel. Because Christ in making him a vessel of election called him a chosen weapon, he is always painted with drawn sword. But not for this is his function of messenger, bearing letters to bring desolation to believers, to be changed, for if he committed scandal by letters, by writing letters he is to teach. If with letters he persecuted, with letters he now defends. Let him suffer with that by which he caused suffering. Let him who by letters wrought death give life by them. God alone can make medicine out of poison.

TOMÁS DE JESÚS
(*c.* 1564–1627)

Little known outside his own country, Tomás de Jesús is one of the most important (and versatile) figures among the Discalced Carmelites of Spain after St. Teresa's death. He was born at Baeza in the south of the Peninsula, a member of the distinguished family of the Dávila, and after brilliant studies in law and theology at Salamanca, received the Carmelite habit at Valladolid in 1586. He early held important office in the Order, being in turn lector at Alcalá and Seville, prior of Zaragoza, and Provincial.

He was attracted to the life of a solitary and in 1592 founded a house where the friars might live the life of hermits either for a time or permanently, in hermitages within the enclosure grounds. Another similar foundation followed in 1599.

Some seven or eight years later, at least his practical interest in this life had to be abandoned, for he was appointed the Pope's ambassador on a special mission to the Congo. Though this embassy did not in point of fact materialize, the appointment meant that Fray Tomás journeyed to Rome and came into personal contact with the Pope, Paul V. He remained for some time in Rome, where he interested himself in the foundation of yet another congregation of Discalced Carmelites, to be concerned with the foreign missions. The Pope approved, but those who wished to dedicate themselves to this task had to take two additional vows:

1. to go wherever they were sent;
2. to refrain from seeking honours or office.

Such provisions would seem eminently reasonable. Various difficulties intervened and it was finally decided that the missionary work of the Order should be handed over to the Italian Congregation—whereupon Tomás de Jesús joined that Congregation! It is more than probable that it was this abortive effort and the writings of Fray Tomás upon the subject of missionary work, which led to the establishment of the Congregation of Propaganda.

The Pope, however, had other work for him and sent him to found houses of Discalced friars in Flanders. We hear of him in Brussels and Louvain in 1610 and 1611, and later in Germany. Other foundations in the Low Countries followed and in 1618 Fray Tomás founded a convent for solitaries near Namur. His old enthusiasm was reasserting itself. The work of the ordinary Discalced foundations went on until 1626 when, owing to ill-health, Tomás de Jesús returned to Rome to Santa Maria della Scala, where he died the following year.

The output of Tomás de Jesús as a writer was considerable. Not all his books were written in Spanish, but with his Latin works we are not here concerned. His two most important spiritual writings are 'Summary and Compendium of the Degrees of Prayer', and the 'Practice of living Faith', this latter being ascetical rather than mystical in character.

The Summary and Compendium was an attempt, based on her writings, to epitomize the teachings of St. Teresa of Jesus. Published with the Summary in the same volume was Tomás de Jesús' 'Treatise on Mental Prayer', summarizing the teachings of saints, doctors and mystical writers on the subject, from which an extract is here given.

OF THE SECOND ACT OR PART OF MENTAL PRAYER,
THE PREPARATION
(from 'Treatise on Mental Prayer')

Immediately the soul places itself before God, the first thing it has to do is to ask his grace to be in his holy presence worthily; and because in the beginning of one's prayer the just man is his own accuser, what he ought then to do is to recognize who he is, contemplating and comparing his lowliness with that immensity and greatness in whose presence he is, considering who God is and who he himself is. This is what St. Francis often repeated: 'Who are you, Lord, and who am I?'—and this with the deepest sincerity he could. Abraham had this knowledge of his lowliness and when he was to speak with God, said: 'How shall I speak with the Lord, when I am dust and ashes?'

To make an examination of conscience also helps in this. Not trusting in yourself, ask our Lord for his grace and help to remain in the presence of His Majesty and to speak and treat with him with fitting reverence. Ask him to send fire from heaven that it may consume the sacrifice which you want to offer him. After having spent some brief time in this, desiring the descent of this divine fire which enkindles and gives light to your heart, and recognizing that if God does not give you this, your efforts are worth nothing and can achieve nothing—then, with great confidence in our Lord, you will be able to move forward into your prayer. But it should be carefully noted that before all things it is fitting that he who gives himself to prayer should rectify the intention. That is, that after having asked God to consume the sacrifice of his prayer, he should resign himself into his hands, saying—'Lord, I place myself here to do your divine will; let what is to your greatest glory be done.' He should esteem himself unworthy that the Lord should hear him and communicate his grace and the gift of prayer to him. If after a good while he remains dry, let him hold it as a great mercy of God that he has allowed him to be in his presence.

This second act of mental prayer, as we said above, is concerned with all that helps in attracting [the divine] goodness. That is, all that helps in disposing the divine will to accept our prayer and petition and to grant us his aid to pray worthily. For this the blessed St. Basil advises that we should not begin our prayer by asking. He proves this from the example of a man who goes to ask some favour from a certain prince—he first tries to extol and praise him and give him thanks for other benefits which he has conferred upon him, and then makes his request. This, he says, we must do in prayer, where the petition should be preceded by that part of prayer which is directed to the divine praise, or giving of thanks for benefits received, or to the recognition of our lowliness and God's greatness—the one for the reason we have given, the other because thereby the will loves God more. Thus this second part of the prayer contains two things. The first is, the giving of thanks, to which belongs the knowledge and appreciation of the benefits received from the hand of God. It behoves us to recognize how wonderful, how precious and how profitable the benefits of our creation, preservation and redemption, and other particular benefits which each one has received have been to us. Likewise we ought to consider with how much love and generosity the author of these benefits, God himself, has conferred them; and, on the other hand, how unworthy and how far we are from deserving them. It also belongs to the giving of thanks, to recognize them, preserve them and respond with due gratitude. The second thing is to exercise oneself in praising and glorifying the Lord, from whose hand we have received such great favours.

Love of praising God arises from consideration of the divine goodness, from admiration of the deep wisdom and of the immensity and sublimity of the power of God. To praise God is to know that he is worthy of all praise and to magnify his power and majesty in reverent wonder. We should consider this power and majesty both in God himself and in all his works, wherein may be found abundant material for divine praise—for it includes not only God himself, but also all his works, which are worthy of all praise.

After this preparation, and before the petition, the saints place the matter of the prayer, which is everything in which the understanding is busied, as it meditates or contemplates. This is usually the life of Christ, our Saviour, hell, judgment, glory, the ugliness of sin, the beauty of virtue, the divine perfections and other similar things, of which we will speak further on. The reason is that in this way these truths are more deeply fixed in the soul, and the will clings more to what it has pondered over more and knows better, and when once the will has become thoroughly roused, one prays with greater fervour. This will be seen when we come more to practical things and the way of making mental prayer, each one of us as he finds best.

JUAN EUSEBIO NIEREMBERG
(c. 1595–1658)

Born in Madrid, Nieremberg was of German origin, being the son of Gottfried Nieremberg, a German who came to Madrid in the suite of Doña María de Austria, daughter of Charles V. Juan Eusebio studied at Alcalá and Salamanca. He was granted a pension by the bishop of Valladolid, and in 1614, to the disgust of his father, entered the Society of Jesus. After completing his studies, he taught Grammar, Natural History and Sacred Scripture. It was Nieremberg who helped Juan de la Cerda to write his commentaries on Tertullian and St. Anselm. The King named him a member of the Commission which was to study the doctrine of the Immaculate Conception. He published many works, including a translation of the *Imitation of Christ*. The most popular of his writings was the *Diferencia entre lo temporal y eterno* (1643). The extract here given is from his 'Letters'.

TO A MOTHER WHO NEGLECTED HER DAUGHTERS FOR HER DEVOTIONS. THE CARRYING OUT OF ONE'S DUTIES IS ENJOINED AS THE FIRST OF ALL DEVOTIONS (Letter 15)

They tell me that you give much edification with your devotion and that you are very happy with its quiet and peace. Provided that God is pleased also, all will be well. But I fear that this will not be altogether the case if your devotion is the indulgence of taste and your quiet, neglect. And it would appear that this is so, for your duty and devotion is the bringing up of your daughters and now they are growing up you think it is sufficient for you to be all day long and even every day in the church, leaving them entirely to servants; but they are not so holy as St. Catherine. Take heed that you do not withdraw from God in seeking him. Do not offend him in trying to please him. The primary devotion ought to be the fulfilment of one's obligations. If these are not fulfilled by one's devotion, it will not be devotion, but pleasure or vanity or delusion. Merit does not consist in quiet alone, sanctity is not in retirement and peace, but in carrying out what God wants and in enduring that. Look after your daughters, even though it mean the loss of peace. Look after your servants too, even if you lose your quietude

and retirement, for this is better than that they should be lost and
you too, for not giving due care to what you ought. You should
realize that there is much self-deception in devotion and tenderness
of affection, even for good things, and that there is a great difference
between pleasurable devotion and the true spirit of that quality.
There are some pious persons who set their pleasure in this, and
to attend to it, fail to carry out other obligations. I knew a person
who, in order to give a lamp to a statue of the Blessed Virgin,
merely for the devotion she felt towards her, failed to pay her
debts to persons in very great need who, since they were not able
to recover what was owing to them from this person, were reduced
to begging for alms. And not seldom does it happen that to celebrate
a feast in honour of a saint, or to give some ornament to a church,
or for some similar thing, people fail to pay the servants and other
debts too.

It will easily be perceived that such devotion is not pure and
that it is more to satisfy one's taste than to give pleasure to God,
whose will is that primarily justice and the other obligations of one's
state of life should be complied with. Even in the works of devotion
themselves, people are wont to fail, omitting to perform the
devotions they originally promised in order to undertake other
new ones they have not promised, pandering to their taste for
novelty. I know of another person who, having made a vow to give
a certain amount of money in alms to a very poor monastery, never
gave it, although he knew the monastery's need, and sent greater
amounts to other monasteries so that they should say Masses,
whereas he had no obligation to do this. All this is to go astray
from the right path. All this is to turn aside from the direction we
have to keep to in what we do, both in regard to men and in regard
to God, that is, following right reason and adjusting ourselves to
our obligations. It is a pity to be condemned for doing good works
and neglecting our obligations. Take heed to your danger, for just
as others fail in justice through performing the devotions of their
taste, it may be that you are failing in piety through not taking
care of your daughters and family.

Do not fail in your obligations. Afterwards, give yourself to
your devotions as much as you like, for I do not tell you not to
perform devotions, but not to put your pleasure in them but in
God; for what follows from your way is that you are not exercising
devotion but pleasure, and I should like you not to have the latter
but to have the former.

When you have adjusted your devotions to your duties, take

heed that there is much more to be done, for just as there is pleasure which seems devotion but is not, so there is devotion that seems to be spiritual and is not so. Not all persons who seem to be spiritual are so, for external devotion is a different thing from the inner spirit. There are many externally devout persons but few who are truly spiritual. There are many who fulfil their obligations, often frequent the sacraments, hear many Masses, fast many days and perform other penances, speak well of spiritual things; but behind all this, they have little of the true spirit of the Gospel, and do not mortify their passions, nor despise themselves and the world. If a word is said to them, they reply angrily. If a misfortune befalls them, they cannot succeed in accepting the will of God. If their honour is touched, they die of grief. If they lay claim to a thing, they lose their peace and desire it with anxiety. They are impatient and querulous; they have vain theories and points of honour, they avenge themselves on occasion, they have superfluous tastes and other similar faults.

The reason is that they are not truly spiritual, they are not rooted in poverty of spirit nor in humility and patience, but content themselves with not committing grave sin and with external exercises of devotion and penance, without really aiming at the interior mortification of the passions. Such persons, although they generally live a long time without committing mortal sin, are not without danger of so doing if something contrary to their taste comes along, for when such an occasion occurs they usually fall. What is most sure is the imitation of Christ in patience, humility and mortification. Try to aspire to this and begin by fulfilling your obligations. Adjust your devotion to them and try to be spiritual and be mortified in your passions and your taste.

TO A PERSON WHO HAD GROWN LUKEWARM IN PRAYER. IT IS EXPLAINED HOW THE SOUL IS TO BE THE TEMPLE OF GOD (Letter 45)

The King of heaven came and dwelt in a manger, because there was no one to receive him on earth. Try to receive him in your house and make a royal dwelling for him in your soul, because he is King, and a house of prayer, because he is God. Consecrate your heart to him as a holy temple, clean and pure. Let there be in it continual sacrifice by mortification and continual prayer through the presence of God. It is pitiful that when the soul of the Christian is the temple of God, people should profane it so much. Some make it a den of robbers, others a house of business, and others a brothel, as Hugo Foilletano said.

Envy and pride often convert the soul from a temple of God into a den of robbers. It begins to murmur about others, setting them in a bad light and, as it were, robbing them of their virtues, calumniating as evil even the good works of others and robbing them of their honour in many ways. Similarly, envy and ambition turn the soul, which is the house of God, into a house of business and traffic, where everything is done from self-interest and ways and schemes of gaining more sought, where nothing is done with a pure intention but only for one's own convenience, what is of obligation not being looked to except when the question of one's own profit is involved. Frivolity and pleasure make a brothel of the soul, allowing entrance to every delight, keeping the gates of all five senses open. Havoc such as this produces vice in souls and profanes the temple of God more wretchedly than Antiochus profaned the temple of Jerusalem; and as the Jews wept to see their temple profaned and destroyed, so might we weep for so many spiritual temples miserably violated and profaned. What great zeal did the Son of God show that all reverence might be paid to the material temple which Herod built. Although he was meekness itself, he was so severely angry with those who there bought and sold the things that were to be offered in sacrifice, that with a whip in his hand he made them give over that occupation, and such a number of people who had gathered together at that season fled from his angry countenance, that they would be sufficient to conquer the world—at least Alexander the Great conquered it with no more numerous army. For this reason certain of the Fathers say that this was either the greatest or among the greatest of the miracles of Jesus Christ, that so many people should flee from a man who was alone and unarmed, for such was the rigour of severity he showed on account of the want of respect paid to the temple of God, that he astonished all.

If Jesus Christ were really to enter into certain souls, what armies of profane thoughts and desires would he find to drive out! May the Son of God enter into us, and with zeal for the glory of the Father and reverence for his holy house, may he drive out from our souls all that is not sanctity and purity and cast down from the altar of our heart the great idol of self-love, so that we may be pure temples, consecrated solely to the true God, with such purity that it is an imitation of what there is in heaven. Because not only ought we to keep ourselves for God as pure temples, but to make ourselves as it were the purest of heavens, so that the Creator of heaven and earth may be and dwell in us with a special presence. It was for this reason that St. Augustine applied those words of the *Pater noster* where it says 'who art in heaven', to the souls of the just, which must be heavens so that the heavenly Father may be in them. Let us aim at this, so that Christ may be born and may be in our heart and not find there the mire of a cattle-shed. Let there not be there the dung of vice nor the straw of human vanities, nor the cobwebs of human schemes and intriguing, but simplicity and purity and three kings who adore him; that is, all three powers of our soul cast down at his feet and employed in his service, offering him the incense of prayer, the myrrh of mortification and the gold of charity.

BALTASAR GRACIÁN
(1601–1658)

Baltasar Gracián was a native of Belmonte, near Calatayud. He was brought up in Toledo by a learned uncle. At the age of eighteen, he entered the Society of Jesus, completing his studies in Calatayud and Zaragoza. He spent some years teaching in Calatayud. After four years' study of theology and ordination, Gracián was professed in 1635. In the time of Philip IV, we read of him as an army chaplain in the wars of Cataluña. He became Rector of the novitiate at Tarragona and held many other important offices.

Gracián is chiefly known as a writer. He first attracted attention as the author of *El Héroe*, perhaps written as a reply to Machiavelli's *Il Principe*. He published this, as he did all his books except *El Comulgatorio*, without the permission of his superiors, and for his disobedience was deprived of the Chair of Sacred Scripture at Zaragoza. He was sent to the Colegio de Graus and afterwards to Tarazona, where he died. The statement sometimes made that he was imprisoned and ill-treated by his Order is quite without foundation.

El Comulgatorio ('On Holy Communion') is Baltasar Gracián's only religious work, yet it is profoundly religious, as the extracts given will show. It was published in Zaragoza in 1655.

'OF THE APPLICATION TO HOLY COMMUNION OF THE FOUNT OF LIVING WATERS WHICH THE LORD OPENED IN THE HEART OF THE SAMARITAN WOMAN'
(*El Comulgatorio*—Meditation XIV)

Point the first:

O Good Jesus! My God and my Lord! In what great thirst you journey in search of a woman so satisfied with her misdeeds! A vile woman, yea, but an unfortunate woman, no, since she meets the fountain of all wealth and riches. Oh how we learn to know you, Lord, to realize how much you value souls, that for one alone you would have done what you did for all! From what a distance have you come to seek her, seeing that you have come down from the highest heaven. I am not surprised to see your sweat pouring down drop by drop, for some day you will sweat blood and streams of it will run down from your wounds. But the Samaritan woman paid no attention to you and yet how much you had her in mind, and in your heart. She, knowing nothing of eternal good, was athirst for pleasures that perish—she went after the broken cisterns and neglected the fountain of living waters. How little did she think to find the true wealth, for she thought only of making herself rich! She came in search of water, a symbol of fugitive delights, and she found the eternal stream of grace.

Soul of mine, the same is happening to you today. You are going about lost in search of slippery pleasures and the Lord is waiting for you, if not at the well of Jacob, at that of the altar, the true and perennial spring of his blood and his grace. Look! Approach with that thirst of yours those five fountains of salvation: allow yourself to be found by him who is searching for you, take advantage of the opportunity and quench the thirst of your desires. Draw out [from these fountains] a true knowledge of his mercy and your misery, of your forgetfulness and his care.

Point the second:

Christ begins to prepare her, to make her capable of receiving his infinite mercies; he comes asking in order to give and he asks her for a drop of water. He, who is to shed all his blood for her, begins by asking a little in order to give much. How he thirsts to give! What desire to communicate his heavenly gifts! With desire I have desired, says the same Lord. Thirsting to satisfy us, he asks for water, but it is of tears that cleanse the soul, that make the conscience pure, that conscience where he is to receive hospitality. He thirsts with longing for us to quench our thirst.

Realize, then, soul of mine, that the same Lord, really and truly present in this divine sacrament, is saying to you: 'Soul, give me to drink. I ask you for tears; have compassion on my thirst which lasted all my life: do not give me the gall of your ingratitude nor the vinegar of your lukewarmness. Let at least one tear fall for so many faults, let the fountains of your eyes be opened when the fountains of my blood are communicated to you in streams.' Drink to your Redeemer with tears of bitterness that he may submerge you in depths of sweetness. Draw forth a great contempt for worldly delights and a great thirst for divine joys, in order eternally to enjoy this perennial stream of grace.

Point the third:

Even to her very Creator the wretched woman denies a drop of water when he asks her for it. What ingratitude! But the Lord is so far from turning his back upon her that he rather takes an opportunity from this to favour her. The Samaritan woman considers that she has sufficient justification for refusing him a little water, like all those who excuse themselves from serving him. Jesus replies, forgetting her disservice to him, for he is intent on our good. 'Woman, if you did but know the gift of God, and to you, and at this hour! If you did but know with whom you are speaking—with me, perennial fount of all good, mine of treasure, source of true consolation—you would ask me, and I would freely give you, not a drop of water, but a whole fountain of well-being and mercies, a fountain which springs up towards heaven and leads to eternal life.'

Hear, daughter. Bend down your ear, soul of mine, for the same Lord says the same thing to you from the altar. Oh, if you did but know! If you could but recognize this gift of gifts, this favour of favours, which today you receive when you receive Communion! If you did but know who this great Lord is whom you are enclosing in your breast! Your only good, the whole of your medicine, your comfort, your happiness, your life and your centre: he who alone can fill your heart and satisfy your desires. How you should ask him for this bread of life, how you should frequent the fount of grace, the table of the altar, with greater fervour. Stir up your faith, set your love ablaze, and throw yourself and your thirst into this abundant fountain of his blood, the thirst-quenching drink of his wounds, and drink your fill, soul, of God.

Point the fourth:

When the Samaritan woman recognizes her Creator and Redeemer, how happily she sets off. From a sinner she has become a preacher! She does not turn her back on the stream ungratefully, but goes away, to return many times over, in gratitude. She goes to communicate to others the good she has received, to repay the mercies shown her in praises, as she congratulates herself on her good fortune. She goes into her village proclaiming aloud that she has found the Messias. There is not enough room in her heart for her happiness, and the first-fruits of her love of God thus overflow on to her neighbours; she summons not now seven only for the purpose of transgression,[1] but all to share her favour.

---

[1] Is this obscure phrase perhaps a reference to 'Thou hast had five husbands and he whom thou now hast is not thy husband'? Five, with 'he whom thou now hast' and the woman herself, would make up seven. Or does it refer to Mary Magdalene, out of whom were cast seven devils?

Think, soul of mine, how much more grateful you ought to show yourself to this Lord, who has freely given you today, not a fountain of water, but all five fountains of his precious blood, so that you are laved deep in his mercies. Be grateful to him and you will be rewarded. Make yourself a herald of his gifts, communicating to all and sharing with all this great good, which for this reason is called Communion.

HOW TO COMMUNICATE WITH THE REVERENCE OF THE SERAPHIM BEFORE THE THRONE OF GOD
(*El Comulgatorio*—Meditation XV)

Point the first:

Contemplate the immense majesty of the infinite and eternal God which, if it cannot be contained within the heaven of heavens, how much less upon this earth of earth. See him surrounded by the winged hierarchies, attended by the spirits around his throne, some loving him, others contemplating him, and all praising and exalting him. Here, indeed, your soul might faint away with greater reason than that queen of the South in Solomon's earthly palace. Turn, then, the eyes of faith to this most divine sacrament and realize how the same Lord who there really and truly occupies that majestic throne of his infinite grandeur, is here circumscribed in this Host with the fullness of love. There immense, here contained within a small space. There his majesty receiving reverence, here his love asking for tokens of friendship.

Consider, if you had to pass through the midst of the angelic hosts, breaking through the winged hierarchies, making a way for yourself between the cherubim and seraphim on this side and on that—with how much reverential awe you would proceed, with what humility you would approach. Think, then, that today you are going to receive the same Lord and God in the midst of the invisible hierarchies. Look to the preparation with which you come, with the wings of what virtue you draw near, and let your preparation emulate that of the cherubim in knowledge and that of the seraphim in love.

Point the second:

The spirits of fire are so near to God's infinite majesty that they are present on the same throne, although always fluttering their wings to draw even nearer, for he who knows God desires him still more. They are on fire in the divine love and therefore are the more bound to God, for love not only permits [approach] but unifies. Great is their love and greater still their desire.

Think here, soul of mine, on your lukewarmness, compare your coldness with that fire, and say how you dare approach with so little fervour a God who is consuming fire? Let the powers of your soul move your understanding to know him, enkindle your will to love him, and this increasingly more and more, so that what the winged spirits do not attain to in their splendour, you may attain to in your lowliness; for not only is it permitted to you to be in the Lord's presence, fluttering your wings, but to touch him with your lips, tasting his sweetness in your mouth, even putting him within your breast. It is granted to the seraphim to be present at the throne of God, you who have the same God present within your very heart have little to envy them for: their knowledge, not their happiness; esteem, but not favour.

Point the third:

The spirits of love veiled their faces, abashed at not loving their Lord and God as much as they ought, as much as they longed to do, because their capacity did not equal their desire; they made a covering with their wings for their bashfulness, if it was not already a veil for their reverence. They were present and, in their confusion at such immediate nearness, were ashamed at their dullness and lack of brightness. They also covered their feet, accusing them of being slow in keeping pace with their wings and of their affections being held back by them.

Slothful soul! Reflect that if the seraphim fear they are unworthy to appear before the immense majesty of God and dread beholding it face to face, you—so full of imperfections if not of faults, so cold in his divine love, so lukewarm in his divine service—are you not covered with confusion at coming to receive him today, when your heart will serve as his throne? The seraphim accuse their feet which are made to tread stars; and you, with feet covered with the mire of the world, covered with the dust of your nothingness, how do you dare to approach? Be ashamed of your baseness. The very kindness of this Sacramental Lord is sufficient to remove your unworthiness; make up with humiliations what you lack in powers, in order to be able to attain to such great favours.

Point the fourth:

The seraphim, recognizing their blessedness, never ceased to praise the divine majesty. Night and day they repeated the Holy,

Holy, Holy, which is the divine escutcheon. In choirs they intoned it, stimulating each other to eternal praise. In uninterrupted canticles they gave the thanks they owed, and with continuous voice they eternally hymned the praises of the Lord.

Learn, soul of mine, from such great masters of love to know how to be grateful. Let your fervour emulate their fire. Let your attentiveness correspond to their continued presence, and if your lack of capacity should hinder you, the favour shown you should encourage you to go forward. Match the depths of your lowliness with delicate expressions of love, the full range of your flight with the modesty of discretion, returning thanks in exchange for favours and exchanging infinite mercies for eternal praise for ever and ever. Amen.

MARÍA DE ÁGREDA
(1602–1665)

María was born in the city by whose name she is known. She was exceptional even from childhood, making a vow of chastity at the age of eight. At twelve she thought of becoming a nun. This ambition she finally achieved at the age of seventeen, and her father—he was sixty-three—mother and sister likewise all entered religion. Her father gave María the money to found the convent of Discalced nuns of the Immaculate Conception, and Franciscan observance, in Ágreda. She became ill through the austerities she practised, but later recovered her health and was elected prioress, an office in which she remained for thirty-five years.

The fame of María de Ágreda's sanctity spread to all parts of the kingdom. Philip IV honoured her with a visit, consulting her about the good of the realm, and for twenty-two years she kept up a correspondence with the King. Her letters show prudence, clear-sightedness and a great sense of justice. Some are ascetical, some political, some moral. Many treat of spiritual perfection.

The 'case' of María of Ágreda was examined by the Inquisition, but she was found to be both blameless and orthodox. She wrote a number of spiritual works—'Meditations on the Passion', 'Litany of Praise to the Mother of God', 'Daily Exercises', and so on. The extract given is from the 'Mystical City of God', her most important book.

THE ASCENSION OF CHRIST OUR REDEEMER
(from 'The Mystical City of God')

That most blissful hour arrived in which the Only-begotten Son of the Eternal Father, who came down from heaven in his Incarnation as man, was to go up there in a wonderful and fitting ascension to sit at the right hand [of the Father], which was his right as heir of his eternity, engendered as he was of his substance in equality and unity of nature and infinite glory. He ascended so high because he first descended to the lower parts of the earth as the Apostle says,[1] leaving all things fulfilled that were said and written, of his coming to the world, his life, death and human redemption. He penetrated as Lord of all to the very centre of the earth; and placed the seal on all his mysteries with that of his Ascension, in which he

---

[1] Ephesians 4:9.

left us the Holy Spirit he had promised, who would not come unless the same Lord first ascended to the heavens, for he, with the Father, was to send him to his new Church. To commemorate this day, so full of joy and mystery, Christ, our good, chose as his special witnesses the one hundred and twenty persons in the Cenacle to whom he joined himself, as was said in the last chapter, and these were most holy Mary and the eleven Apostles, the seventy-two disciples, Mary Magdalene, Martha and Lazarus their brother, and the other Marys and certain of the faithful, both men and women, until the above-mentioned number of one hundred and twenty was completed.

With this little flock our divine shepherd Jesus went forth from the Upper Room, taking them all through the streets of Jerusalem, and at his side walked his most blessed Mother. Then the Apostles and all the others went towards Bethany, which was less than half a league away from the Mount of Olives. The company of angels and saints who came forth from limbo and purgatory followed him triumphant and victorious with new songs of praise, although only most holy Mary enjoyed the sight of him. The Resurrection of Jesus the Nazarene was already spread abroad through all Jerusalem and Palestine, although the perfidious malice of the chief priests tried to make people believe the false statement that his disciples had stolen him away[1]; but many neither admitted it nor gave it credence. With all this divine Providence arranged that none of the dwellers in the city who were either incredulous or doubting should notice that holy procession that went forth from the Upper Room, or should hinder it on its way. None was aware of it, and justly so, for they were incapable of perceiving such a marvellous mystery, notwithstanding the fact that Jesus, the captain and master, was invisible to all the others except the hundred and twenty just, whom he chose, that they might see him ascend to heaven.

With assurance that the power of the Lord himself was going before them, they all went on their way until they reached the highest point of Mount Olivet. Arriving at the place determined upon, they formed three bands, one of angels, another of saints, and the third of the Apostles and the faithful, who were divided into two columns, and Christ our Saviour formed the head. Then the most prudent Mother prostrated herself at the feet of her Son, and adored him as true God and Redeemer of the world, with wonderful reverence and humility, and asked him for his last

[1] Cf. Matthew 28:13.

blessing. All the rest of the faithful who were there did the same in imitation of their great Queen, and with tears of longing asked the Lord if at that time he was to restore the Kingdom of Israel.[1] His Majesty answered them that that secret was his eternal Father's and it was not fitting for them to know it, and that what at that time was necessary and fitting was that when they had received the Holy Spirit, they should preach in Jerusalem, in Samaria, and throughout the world the mysteries of mankind's redemption.

When His Divine Majesty had bid farewell to that holy and happy gathering of faithful souls with peaceful and majestic countenance, he joined his hands and of his own power began to rise from the ground, leaving on it the marks or imprints of his sacred feet. With a very gentle movement, he went his way into the region of the air, leaving behind him the [longing] eyes and hearts of those first-born sons, who amid sighs and tears followed him with their love.

[1] Acts 1:6–8.